CONTENTS

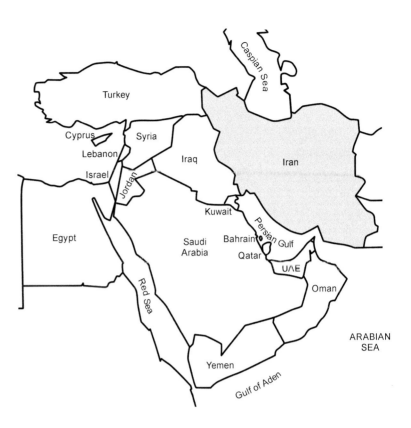

Helion & Company Limited
26 Willow Road
Solihull
West Midlands
B91 1UE
England
Tel. 0121 705 3393
Fax 0121 711 4075
Email: info@helion.co.uk
Website: www.helion.co.uk
Twitter: @helionbooks
Visit our blog http://blog.helion.co.uk/

Published by Helion & Company 2015
Designed and typeset by Kerrin Cocks, SA Publishing Services
Cover designed by Farr out Publications, Wokingham, Berkshire
Aircraft artwork in colour section © Tom Cooper
Printed by Henry Ling Ltd, Dorchester, Dorset

Text © Babak Taghvaee 2015
Images © as individually credited
Maps drawn by George Anderson © Helion & Company Ltd 2015

ISBN 978-1-910294-13-0

British Library Cataloguing-in-Publication Data.
A catalogue record for this book is available from the British Library.

For details of other military history titles published by Helion & Company
Limited contact the above address, or visit our website: http://www.helion.co.uk.

We always welcome receiving book proposals from prospective authors.

Acknowledgements

I would like to express my gratitude to many people who helped me with the research for this book; specifically Major Farhad Nassirkhani (IIAF, ret.), Brigadier-General Ahmad Mehrniya (IRIAF, ret.), Brigadier-General Alireza Namaki-Araghi (IRIAF), Brigadier-General Iraj Amir-Jalali (IRIAF, ret.), Master Sergeant Ali Gholam-Ali (IRIAF, ret.) and Brigadier-General Ahmad Sadik (IrAF, ret.). There are those whom I am unable to mention by name out of concern for their and their families' safety. Further to this, I would like to thank Tom Cooper, Dr Heinz Berger, Marco Dijkshoorn, Leon Manuchehrian, Claudio Maranta, Marinus Dirk-Tabak and Andreas Rupprecht for their generous assistance with information, the reconstruction of specific events and sharing photographs from their private collections.

Glossary

AB air base

AB/AS Agusta-Bell or Agusta-Sikorsky (Italian helicopter manufacturer)

AFB air force base

AIM air-intercept missile (standardized US military designation for air-to-air missiles)

ASW anti-surface/submarine warfare

AWACS Airborne Early Warning Control System

CAP combat air patrol

CAS close air support

CBU Cluster Bomb Unit

C-in-C commander-in-chief

CENTO Central Treaty Organization

CO commanding officer

COIN counter-insurgent or counter-insurgency

Col colonel

CP command post

CSAR Combat Search and Rescue

DHC de Havilland Canada (aircraft manufacturer)

ECM electronic countermeasures

ELINT electronic intelligence

FAE fuel-air explosives (weapon type)

FCF functional check flight

Fencer ASCC code for Su-24 jet fighter-bomber

FMS foreign military sales [programme]

FS fighter squadron

Gen general

HAF Hellenic Air Force

HQ headquarters

IACI Iranian Aircraft Industries

IAP international airport

IIAA Imperial Iranian Army Aviation (official designation until 1979)

IIAF Imperial Iranian Air Force (official designation from 1924 until 1979)

IINA Imperial Iranian Naval Aviation (official designation until 1979)

INS internal navigation system

IrAAC Iraqi Army Aviation Corps

IrAF Iraqi Air Force

IRGC Islamic Revolutionary Guards Corps (Iranian militia originally organized in support of the newly emerging Islamic government of Iran; popularly known as Pasdaran, but including other militia and branches as well)

IRIAA Islamic Republic of Iran Army Aviation (official designation since 1979)

IRIAF Islamic Republic of Iran Air Force (official designation since 1979)

IRINA Islamic Republic of Iran Naval Aviation (official designation since 1979)

KIA killed in action

km kilometre

LGB laser-guided bomb

Lt lieutenant

Lt-Col lieutenant-colonel

MAAG Military Advisory Assistance Group [USA]

Maj major

Maj-Gen major-general

MANPAD man-portable air defence (light, surface-to-air missiles that can be carried and deployed in combat by a single soldier)

MAP Military Assistance Programme

MiG Mikoyan i Gurevich (the design bureau led by Artyom Ivanovich Mikoyan and Mikhail Iosifovich Gurevich, also known as OKB-155 or MMZ Zenit)

NATO North Atlantic Treaty Organization

QRA Quick Reaction Alert

RJAF Royal Jordanian Air Force

SAM surface-to-air missile

SAR search and rescue

SAVAK Iranian Organization of Intelligence and National Security

SIGINT signals intelligence

SSJD Self-Sufficiency Jihad Division

SVAF South Vietnamese Air Force

TACAN tactical air navigation system

TAB tactical air base

TAS transport aircraft squadron

TFB tactical fighter base

TuAF Türk Hava Kuvvetleri (Turkish Air Force)

TFS tactical fighter squadron

USD US Dollar

USSR Union of Soviet Socialist Republics

VIP very important person

Introduction

Iran, the land of Pars, the land of Persian kings, one of the world's most ancient civilizations and oldest, continuously existing countries, has played a prominent role on the international scene through history. The ancient empires of the Achaemenids, Parthias and Sassanids were dominating powers in western Asia, the Middle East, North Africa and southeastern Europe through the centuries. Arab and Mongol invasions gradually destroyed this status. The restoration of its former power and glory became the primary issue for many subsequent Persian kings, including the Reza Shah Pahlavi and his son, Mohammad Reza Shah Pahlavi, the last royal rulers of the country.

While attempting to reunite their country and rebuild the nation – moving Iran toward modernism and the introduction of the rule of law – they found themselves under threat from all corners of the country. So much so that Reza Shah was removed by the combined British-Soviet invasion of 1941.

Subsequently his son found himself under similar pressures and hostilities. State security became a paramount issue for the young ruler. Bolstered by the nationalization of Iranian oil and gas resources he began investing ever-larger sums of money – first for acquiring and establishing military forces that became a powerful deterrent to foreign and domestic enemies, and then for acquiring the technology and expertise that would shape his country into a major industrial power in the Middle East.

It was against this backdrop that Iran became the biggest export customer for Northrop's unique F-5A/B Freedom Fighter, a lightweight jet fighter, and then the F-5E/F Tiger II in the 1960s and 70s. It was also at this juncture that the then Imperial Iranian Air Force (IIAF), not only purchased over 300 such aircraft, but also the infrastructure necessary to operate them and maintain them, their equipment and manufacture weapons for them too.

The popular unrest that conflagrated into the Islamic Revolution of 1978–79 and resulted in the downfall of the Pahlavi dynasty and changed everything. The new government established itself as an autocracy of traditional clerical leaders, supported by an uneducated civil society. These not only cut their ties to the USA but turned the country into a staunch enemy of the West in general. Iranian armed forces suddenly faced massive budget cuts and the cancellation of most foreign military agreements. Thereafter it was subject to a series of ideologically motivated purges, rendering the country defenceless and again exposing it to its foreign enemies.

It was precisely this resultant weakness – and specifically that of its air force, renamed the Islamic Republic of Iran Air Force (IRIAF) in 1979 – that prompted its arch enemy Iraq to invade on 22 September 1980. It was in this fashion that six squadrons equipped with F-5s became embroiled in a war that was to last eight years.

This book is about the relentless efforts of Iranian pilots and ground crew, the heroism of the men who defended the territorial integrity of their nation against challenging odds while deploying the workhorse of their air force – Northrop's F-5 – in thousands of combat sorties. Iranian F-5s have flown all sorts of missions, from combat air patrols (CAPs), close-air-support (CAS), interdiction-strikes and reconnaissance. There is no doubt that they brought the Iraqi invasion to its knees; there is also little doubt that they caused heavy enemy casualties. However, lacking advanced electronic equipment for self-protection and medium-range, air-to-air missiles (MRAAMs) in the face of the full spectrum of Iraqi weapons, the crews and their aircraft suffered extensively: 49 percent of the F-5s available in 1979 and 46 percent of their pilots were lost in that war.

The war between Iran and Iraq ended when – facing immense economic and political pressures – the Iranian government accepted a UN-negotiated ceasefire in 1988. By that time, what was left of the IRIAF's F-5 fleet and its personnel was exhausted and in tatters.

After eight years of intensive warfare that called for extensive air support, the air force – in cooperation with personnel from its own maintenance depots and civilian institutions – managed to keep its F-5s operational and maintained. However, the surviving aircraft were in need of major overhauls and upgrades and there was an urgent need to replace losses.

The establishment of institutions such as the Self-Sufficiency Jihad group and Owj Industries during the later stages of the Iran–Iraq war proved crucial for Iran's ability to locally produce spare parts and provide the impetus for the creation of indigenous variants of the F-5. Due to plenty of hard work, often disrupted and constrained by insufficient funding and problems related to the lack of industrial management skills, such institutions and companies enabled the air force to retain its surviving fleet of F-5s through the 1990s, and made it possible to deploy them in subsequent conflicts, primarily related to voilatile situations in Afghanistan.

Now, 47 years after the first Northrop F-5A/Bs entered service in Iran, 39 years after the delivery of the first F-5E/Fs and nearly 20 years after their originally scheduled replacement date, five sub-variants of these two types remain in service with the air force and represent no less than 33.5 percent of its total fighter force. Aside from constituting major fire power of the four frontline squadrons at three air bases, they are also used as advanced trainers. There is little doubt that the fleet is in urgent need of an upgrade, if not an outright replacement. However, this is unlikely to happen in the near future, although it seems that despite this the F-5 is to remain in service with the IRIAF for many years.

Chapter One
HOW IT BEGAN

The origin of the Iranian air force can be traced back to the early 1920s when an air office was established within the Iranian army headquarters (HQs) to assess the possibility of establishing an air arm. Equipped with a miscellany of light transports and reconnaissance bombers purchased from Germany and the USSR and flown by Iranian pilots trained abroad, the resulting Army Cooperation Unit was officially established on 1 June 1924 at Ghaleh-Morghi airfield, then outside Tehran. This date was celebrated as Air Force Day until 1979.

By 1932 the army aviation branch had been expanded and reorganized as the Imperial Iranian Air Force. Supported by a nascent aviation industry, this branch grew in size and importance to the point where its inventory amounted to 283 aircraft organized in 11 wings and 24 squadrons based at five airfields by 1940. Plans for further expansion were interrupted in 1941 when Iran was invaded by British and Soviet military forces, almost totally disarming its military forces

Following the withdrawal of the British and Soviet occupation forces after the Second World War the Iranian government launched an all-out campaign to rebuild its military, including the IIAF. Due to poor economic conditions, and because the British and Soviets continued fostering ethnic conflicts and separatist movements in Azerbaijan, Kurdistan, Fars, Lorestan and other Iranian provinces, this proved anything but easy. Dedicated to the prevention of the dissolution of his country, the young Shah Mohammad Reza Pahlavi was forced to fight low-scale, counter-insurgency (COIN) wars while simultaneously rebuilding his military.

In 1948 the IIAF situation was left wanting with 191 outdated and mostly unserviceable aircraft available to it. Its inventory included Hawker Furies, Audaxes, Hinds and de Havilland Tiger Moths. These 'combat assets' were supported by a miscellany of Junkers W-33 and de Havilland DH.89 Dragon Rapide light bombers and transports. The most modern combat aircraft in service were 30 Hawker Hurricane Mk.IICs ordered in 1939 and eventually delivered in 1946–47.

Facing the threat of Soviet-supported communist insurgency, the Shah turned to the USA for help and – after Iranian armed forces successfully concluded Operation Freedom Azerbaijan and prevented the secession of that province – Washington reverted positively. It was in this way that the Iranian government received its first major package of military aid from the USA in 1949–50: 60 Republic P-47D Thunderbolt fighters, seven Douglas C-47A Skytrain transports, 36 Piper L-4H liaison aircraft, 15 Stearman PT-13D Kaydet primary trainers and 30 North American AT-6D light strikers. As such, several fighter regiments, bomber and reconnaissance squadrons, transport squadrons and training units were rebuilt or reformed in Tehran, Mashhad, Isfahan, Shiraz and Ahwaz.

The US continued to provide military aid during the next year, including 32 Lockheed T-33A jet trainers and 75 Republic F-84G Thunderjet fighter-bombers, delivered between 1955 and 1957, and 52 North American F-86F Sabres by 1960. Deliveries of jet fighters prompted the IIAF to launch its first major expansion programme which included the construction of new air bases and the establishment and re-equipment of a number of new units. Vahdati, a newly constructed air base located outside the town of Dezful in southwestern Iran, was financed by the USA and constructed by the MKO company. It was officially inaugurated on 24 May 1961.

Throughout this period the IIAF experienced no shortages of qualified personnel. The service had retained enough pilots and technicians during the years of occupation and additional personnel were trained in Iran and abroad during the following years. Between 1957 and 1960 further training programmes were launched to increase the number of skilled pilots and technicians, resulting in high states of readiness for all available aircraft. The IIAF was never challenged when undertaking the full spectrum of operational exercises: all pilots underwent weekly training in gunnery, use of rockets and bombs and – starting in 1960 – deployment of US-made AIM-9B Sidewinder air-to-air missiles (AAMs), the first of which were delivered two years later. Despite some problems caused by a lack of necessary ammunition – reorganization only happened in the IIAF's combat brigades – the IIAF was operating a total of five squadrons equipped with jets, and during the following year proved capable of deploying four F-86Fs (serials 3-133, 3-140, 3-146 and 3-150) from its 103rd Tactical Fighter Squadron (TFS) to the Democratic Republic of the Congo in support of UN operations there.

NEW REQUIREMENTS

The USSR threat was not the only one Iran faced. In 1958 a bloody revolution removed King Faysal of Iraq, resulting in the establishment of a pan-Arabism government with strong links to Moscow. During the following years much of the Iraqi military was re-equipped with Soviet-made weapons, including 11 Ilyushin Il-28 bombers, and 19 Mikoyan i Gurevich MiG-15 and 17 MiG-17F jet fighters. East of Iran, Afghanistan was maintaining friendly relations with the USSR too, and its air force was equipped with no less than 46 Il-28s and around 100 MiGs between 1957 and 1959. By 1960 Iraq began receiving the first of 14 MiG-19s and was negotiating the acquisition of 36 MiG-19PMs, equipped with the PR-2U radar, and 100 RS-2US AAMs. Although the Soviets began delivering the MiG-19PMs they never entered service in the Iraqi Air Force (IrAF), because – as the Iranian Organization of Intelligence and National Security (SAVAK) learned in 1961 – the commanders of the latter were already negotiating for 14 far more superior MiG-21 interceptors armed with R-3S missiles (the Soviet version of the US-made AIM-9B Sidewinder) and 10 Tupolev Tu-16 medium bombers. This sounded alarm bells in Iran and the government immediately started ordering corresponding armament.

In 1960 the IIAF high command understood that the available F-86Fs were insufficient to provide effective defence of Iranian airspace. Since the Shah had already befriended the CEO of Northrop Aircraft Manufacturing Corporation, Tom Jones, the Iranians found it relatively easy to accept the US proposal for supplies of Northrop's new lightweight fighter design, designated F-5A Freedom Fighter, as a supplement to the F-86.

The Iranians agreed with this proposal but expressed their desire to replace the F-86s with something superior. The Shah and his IIAF commanders had strongly favoured the then new McDonnell Douglas F-4 Phantom II interceptor – its US Air Force (USAF) variant designated the F-110. During a meeting between Iranian and US officials held in Tehran on 19 September 1962, Mohammad Reza Shah Pahlavi impressed upon the US ambassador to Iran, Julius C. Holmes, chief of the US military assistance group in Iran, Major-General John C. Hayden and the representative of the US office of chairman Joint Chiefs of Staff, Brigadier-General H. A. Twitchell,

Shah Mohammad Reza Pahlavi seen before his test flight on a F-5B at Los Angeles on 10 June 1964. He was a highly skilled aviator and pilot, trained on – among others – the Hawker Hurricane fighter, Boeing B-17G Flying Fortress, the C-47 and Avro Anson transports, and a number of helicopter types. (Babak Taghvaee Collection)

IIAF commnder-in-chief, Brigadier-General Mohammad Khatami after his flight onboard F-5B 63-08445 at Mehrabad International Airport on 1 August 1964. (Babak Taghvaee Collection)

the need for the IIAF to be equipped with F-110s because only they would offer the capability necessary to intercept the threat projected by Iraqi Tu-16s. Correspondingly, the Iranian head of state openly asked if Washington would be ready to provide McDonnell Douglas F-110 Phantom II (the USAF's designation for what was originally a US Navy project, F-4; later redesignated F-4C) instead of F-5s. Since the F-110 were expensive and sophisticated aircraft, not planned for export at that time, the Americans turned the request down. Eventually, an agreement was reached for the USA to provide the F-5 as a low-cost and low-maintenance alternative for the IIAF.

In June 1964 Northrop invited the Shah to visit the USA and watch

a demonstration flight of the F-5A prototype. The Shah accepted and was given an opportunity to fly the F-5B two-seater conversion trainer from an air base near Los Angeles. During the course of subsequent negotiations with representatives of the US military, the Shah – who not only held a licence but had been an accomplished pilot since the 1940s – concluded that the F-5 proved a 'beautiful plane, highly manoeuvrable, very easy to fly, and with substantially better characteristics than he had understood'. While US negotiators admitted that the MiG-21 was in certain aspects superior to the F-5A, they observed that its short range would prevent it from effectively operating against Northrop's fighter anywhere inside Iranian airspace. This, in turn, would mean that if acquired by the IIAF, the F-5A would be free to handle Iraqi Tu-16s on its own. Impressed by this frank observation the Shah decided against acquiring the F-110, despite its obvious superiority to Northrop's product. A decision was taken for the IIAF to be re-equipped with F-5s – although even then the Shah insisted the deliveries were on condition that the US defence provide better AAMs than those presently available, the AIM-9Bs.[*]

PROJECT PEACE ENFORCER

A final agreement over the acquisition of F-5s by Iran between Tehran and Washington was reached on 4 July 1964. Project Peace Enforcer would see deliveries of 52 F-5As and F-5Bs between 1965 and 1969 of which 26 would be credited within the US-run Military Assistance Programme (MAP), while 26 would be funded by Iran through the Foreign Military Sales (FMS) programme. Following the acquisition of these 52 aircraft, Washington showed a readiness to fund 13 RF-5As and 26 additional F-5A/Bs through MAP, while offering the Iranian government the option to purchase 39 more Freedom Fighters. Each F-5 cost US$756,000, which covered expenses for the airframe, avionics, two engines and internal armament. Drop tanks, five pylons and other external equipment were priced at an additional US$100,000 per plane. The value of Project Peace Enforcer was US$250 million, to be provided between 1965 and 1969. Two hundred million was repayable over a ten-year period, while remaining 50 million would to be in cash and primarily spent on buying spare parts.[†]

On 1 August 1964 Northrop sent its F-5B (serial 63-08445/FA-445, c/n N8008) demonstrator to Tehran. The plane was flown the next day by several high-ranking IIAF commanders, including Brigadier-General Mohammed Khatami.

Training of IIAF personnel on the new type had already begun, in February 1964, when the first group of 50 experienced F-86 pilots

---

[*] The Iranian request for better AAMs was apparently related to the IIAF's request for F-5s compatible with AGM-12 Bullpup-guided air-to-ground missiles. These were promoted by Northrop as part of that type's equipment, but corresponding Iranian demands were turned down by Washington. Indeed, the Americans continued turning down similar Iranian requests during the subsequent years, including one demand for deliveries of correspondingly equipped F-5Cs.

[†] According to available Iranian documentation, Project Peace Enforcer and its related funding was not solely for F-5s. Credit would enable Iran to acquire enough US-made equipment to establish seven infantry divisions, one armoured division – equipped with US-made M60A1 main battle tanks – one special forces group, two airborne battalions and an aviation battalion – equipped with 17 Kaman HH-43 Huskie helicopters and 18 Cessna U-17A utility aircraft. Furthermore, except for acquiring enough F-5s to equip a eight squadrons, the IIAF would purchase an airborne control and warning system (AC&W), enough Lockheed C-130 Hercules transports for three squadrons and a battalion of MIM-23 Hawk surface-to-air missiles (SAMs).

and 200 ground crew personnel arrived at Williams AFB in Arizona to start a conversion course with the 4441st Combat Command Training Squadron USAF. Several pilots then underwent courses at the USAF Fighter Weapons School at Nellis AFB in Nevada, with the aim of preparing themselves to establish a similar institution at Vahdati AB in Iran.

DELIVERY

Training of the first group of F-5 pilots was still underway when Northrop prepared the first 11 F-5As (serialled 63-08383 to 63-08392) and three F-5Bs (serialled 63-8444, 63-8446, and 63-8447) for delivery. Officially handed over to IIAF representatives at Brookley AFB in Alabama on 4 December 1963, the aircraft were flown to Iran by US pilots and arrived at Mehrabad on 12 January 1965. Upon arrival the IIAF personnel replaced all USAF markings with IIAF signage. As ordered by the deputy commander IIAF (logistics), they received serial numbers in range 3-2xx: 3-200 to 3-210 for F-5As and 3-211 to 3-213 for F-5Bs. These first 14 Freedom Fighters officially entered service with the newly established 103rd TFS on 1 February 1965.

The second IIAF unit to convert to F-5s was the 101st TFS, then also based at Mehrabad. By the time this unit became operational the air force was already running conversion courses in Iran – including gunnery- and weapons-delivery training at Kushk-e-Nosrat airfield. This was administered by the second group of Iranian F-5 pilots who served with the third IIAF F-5-unit, the Vahdati-based 203rd Tactical Training Squadron (TTS). Actually, the establishment of the latter unit would experience a series of postponements. Originally scheduled to be equipped with 42 F-86Fs, overhauled by Bedek Aviation company in Israel, in 1965 and 1966, the unit lacked the F-5Bs necessary to enable it to train enough pilots. The IIAF therefore requested delivery of five additional F-5Bs but Washington was only able to grant one (serial 67-22557). It turned out that the USAF was too busy converting dozens of South Vietnamese Air Force pilots to the same type. Because of this, several groups of IIAF pilots had to undergo their gunnery training on Lockheed AT-33As and F-86Fs in Pakistan.

The second batch of F-5s arrived in Iran during the summer of 1965. It consisted of seven F-5As (serials 64-13354 to 64-13360) and two F-5Bs (serials 64-13385 and 64-12286). During the first operational year by the IIAF the F-5s reached an operational readiness rate of 94 percent that increased to 97 percent during 1966.

SHAHROKI AIR BASE: NEW HOME FOR FREEDOM FIGHTERS

By the time the deliveries of F-5s to Iran commenced, the US$10.7 million construction work on TFB.3 outside the city of

Major Gheidian, one of the best Iranian F-86F pilots and commander of one of their squadrons is seen during the removal of the USAF's markings from the F-5A serialled 63-08382 during an official ceremony at Mehrabad IAP on 1 February 1965. (Babak Taghvaee Collection)

In November 1965 a reporter from *Flying* magazine visited the 101st TFS F-5s at TFB.1 Mehrabad and took several photos of them. These photos, were published in the December 1965 issue of the magazine. (*Flying Review* via Tom Cooper)

Major Gheidian (centre), Captain Bahman Forghani (right) – RT-33A pilot at the time – and Brigadier Asre Jadid (left), during the delivery of F-5s in January 1965. A USAF C-5A can be seen in the background. (Babak Taghvaee Collection)

3-405 and 3-409, two of the 101st TFS F-5As seen during routine maintenance while SUU-20 training pods are loaded. (*Flying Review* via Tom Cooper)

IIAF's F-5A 3-402 (c/n: N6025), Brigadier-General Mohammad Khatami (centre), General Nader Jahanbani (left), with personnel at Mehrabad in 1965. (via Tom Cooper)

This photo is taken from a 101st TFS F-5A, serialled 3-514 (c/n: N.6499), over Noushahr in 1969 during a CAP mission over Iranian northern shores near the Caspian Sea. (via Brigadier-General Iraj Amir-Jalali)

Hamedan was nearly complete. Designed and constructed with the air defence of Iran's borders with Iraq in mind, the new air base was named Shahroki, after Colonel Nasrollah Shahroki, killed in a T-33A crash (serial 2-11) near Hamedan, on 13 October 1960. It was envisaged that it would become home to three squadrons equipped with 13 F-5s each. Actually, only the 301st and the 302nd TFS were ever based there, both were established in March 1966.

Most of the aircraft that entered service with these two units belonged to a batch of 14 F-5As (serials 65-10482 to 65-10544) and two F-5Bs (serials 65-10587 and 65-10588) delivered to Iran on 15 January 1966. Contrary to standard practice, they were flown to Iran by US and Iranian pilots. Only 15 out of the 16 aircraft reached their destination, and then one – probably serial number 65-10483 – experienced engine failure and crashed during an

Top left: This photo was taken from TFB.3 Shahrokhi on the day of its official opening in 1965. A USAF C-54 and C-130B belonging to the US Military Advisory Assistance Group (MAAG), one IIAF C-130B, two C-47As, an F-5A and an F-5B can be seen on the ramp during the official ceremony.
(Babak Taghvaee)

Below left: The funeral of Captain Heshmatollah Karim-Zadeh Sirjani on 17 January 1965. General Irfan Tansel, commander-in-chief of the Turkish Air Force (TuAF), is carrying the coffin on his shoulder at TuAF Air Base at Ankara.
(Babak Taghvaee Collection)

Colonel Nasrollah Shahrokhi, killed in a T-33A crash (serialled 2-11) near Hamedan on 13 October 1960. (Babak Taghvaee Collection)

attempted emergency landing at Adana AB in Turkey, killing its pilot, Captain Heshmatollah Krim-Zadeh Sirjani.

The fourth batch of eleven F-5As and five F-5Bs was to enter service with the 102nd TFS. Their deliveries commenced in late 1966 and continued through early 1967. The fifth batch consisted of eleven F-5As and one F-5B, and was delivered during 1968. Most of the aircraft were used to replace the remaining F-86Fs of the 201st TFS at Vahdati, but four were set aside by the IIAF's display team Taj Talee (Golden Crown), which performed publically for the first time with this aircraft on 17 October 1968.

During the same year the IIAF also received 13 RF-5As. These were provided to Iran within the scope of Operation Dark Gene, administered in cooperation with the US National Security Agency (NSA), Central Intelligence Agency (CIA) and SAVAK, apparently with the aim of finding secure routes into the Soviet Union, Iraq and even the Kingdom of Saudi Arabia's airspace.* All IIAF RF-5A pilots were experienced operators of Lockheed RT-33As. After returning from conversion courses in the USA they established the 101st Tactical Reconnaissance Squadron.

Also in 1968 Tehran ordered 13 more F-5A/Bs (priced at US$15

The seventh RF-5A manufactured for the IIAF. This Freedom Fighter, serial 2-254, was the personal aircraft of the CO of the 101st TRS, Colonel Iraj Amir Jalali. This photo was taken by another RF-5A pilot while Jalali was flying above the Port of Pahlavi, along the shores of the Caspian Sea. (via Brigadier-General Iraj Amir Jalali)

---

* The precise nature – even the exact designation – of this operation remains obscure. No relevant Iranian documentation can be located and all inquiries under the US Freedom of Information Act by other researchers have been turned down.

The IIAF performs aerobatics for first time at an anniversary celebration on 17 October 1968. Four F-5As performed while the Shah was at TFB.3. Colonel Amir-Hossein Rabii and Major Mahmoud Imanian can be seen behind him. Three pilots from the Golden Crown Aerobatic Display Team are in front of 3-459. (Babak Taghvaee Collection)

million), planning to station them at an air base that was then under construction on a fertile peninsula outside the port of Bushehr on the coast of the Persian Gulf. Originally, the IIAF requested that these aircraft be equipped with a radar and be compatible with AIM-7C Sparrow AAMs. However, Northrop explained that the necessary technology was not available; therefore these aircraft were delivered as 'standard' F-5A/Bs in 1971, replacing the last F-86Fs.

INTERNATIONAL EXERCISES AND ACCIDENTS

With the IIAF F-5 fleet declared combat ready it was soon put to the test by various exercises supervised by the Central Treaty Organization (CENTO) – a mutual defence treaty originally signed by Iraq and Turkey on 24 February 1955, but later joined by Great Britain, Pakistan and Iran, and supported by the USA (Iraq withdrew from this pact in 1958). During the course of their first related deployment, 14 F-5As and one F-5B from the 302nd TFS – supported by three C-130Hs – visited Sharjah airfield, in the Emirate of Abu Dhabi on 31 March 1967. Later that year, they also participated in a CENTO exercise administered from the Royal Air Force's base on Cyprus in the Mediterranean.[*]

Contrary to IIAF experiences with earlier and aged US-supplied aircraft, especially the P-47 Thunderbolts and F-84 Thunderjets, Iranian F-5s experienced relatively few accidents during their early service. Indeed, throughout the 1960s, only three critical accidents

---

[*] Due to political instability and mutual disagreements, members of the CENTO pact have never established a unified command system like the members of NATO and frequently failed to heed calls for help from member states. An example of this is when Pakistan found itself at odds with India in 1965 and 1971. Nevertheless, Iran did attempt to provide support for its eastern neighbour. In 1968, the Iranian government purchased 98 Canadair-built Sabres from Germany and then sent them to Pakistan, supposedly for overhauls. Of course, the aircraft in question were never returned. Similarly, during the Indo-Pakistani War of 1971, the IIAF supplied three F-5As to Pakistan. These were disassembled and packed for delivery via Turkey on 26 December that year, but only arrived in Pakistan after that war ended with a ceasefire.

Colonel Iraj Amir Jalali (later brigadier-general), commander of the 101st TRS which was later redesignated the 11th TRS, is seen in front of an RF-5A, serialled 2-260 (c/n: RF.1013). He later became commander of TFB.4 Vahdati and then minister of defence. He passed away in 2012 in Tehran. (via Brigadier-General Iraj Amir-Jalali)

are documented, only one of which – the abovementioned crash in Turkey – was fatal. In August 1968, 2nd Lieutenant Gholam Hossein Sadeghi from the 202nd TFS experienced an engine failure while returning to Vahdati AB from a routine training exercise. Sadeghi landed safely; subsequent investigation showed that the leading edge of the aircraft's diffuser liner had a crack (caused by over-use) which had caused the fuel to spread irregularly around the afterburner section of the engine.

Early on the morning of 14 March 1969 the F-5As flown by Captain Nahid and 2nd Lieutenant Riahi made safe emergency landings – as a result of by bad weather – on the road connecting Masshahd with Ghouchan. Both aircraft were subsequently refuelled and flown to Mashhad where the F-5s from TFB.1 maintained a regular presence in order to fly CAPs along the border with the Soviet Union.

Correspondingly, the status of the fleet was still excellent by the time it received a major boost through delivery of 31 F-5As and four F-5Bs in 1969. The aircraft in question were distributed between the 202nd TFS (where they replaced the F-86Fs) and the now established – 203rd TTS, while some were used to establish the 303rd TFS based at Shahroki. By that time the IIAF was already in the process of acquiring F-4Ds which entered service with the 101st and 102nd TFSs, and thus had plenty of surplus airframes that were redistributed to other units.

Top: Standing from left: Major Abdolmolok, commander of 301st TFS and his deputy, Major Mostafa Afshar. Sitting from left: Baratpour, unknown, Shafaghi and Abbas Nejadi during IIAF's gunnery competitions of 1969 at TFB.3. (Babak Taghvaee Collection)

Centre: Captain Mostafa Afshar lifiting up Major Abdolmoluk after becoming top gun during IIAF's gunnery competitions of 1969. (Babak Taghvaee Collection)

Bottom: Technicians of TFB.3 before a FCF of F-5A 3-486 (c/n: N6441) after a maintenance job on 8 September, 1970. Parviz Ramin, one of the air base mechanics, is seen to the left of the pilot. (via Parviz Ramin)

Additional F-5s were sorely needed; the air force was in the process of establishing new air bases – one in Bushehr and another in Tabriz – constructed in cooperation between the IIAF's deputy of logistics and support, the Iranian TSA construction company, and Israeli and US contractors. The base near Bushehr was 80 percent complete at its inauguration as TFB.6 in 1970, by which time the newly established 601st TFS was based there. As of that year, the IIAF was in possession of 96 F-5A/Bs, with 10 F-5As and six F-5Bs still on order.

In 1971 TFB.5 was completed outside Tabriz and one F-5-squadron based there with delivery of the final batch of 17 F-5As and nine F-5Bs during the same year. Project Peace Enforcer was finally complete.

ARVAND RÜD: FIRST (NEAR) COMBAT EXPERIENCE

1969 brought with it the first opportunity for the IIAF's F-5s to taste combat. In April that year, the government of Iraq unilaterally closed the Arvand Rüd waterway (the lower part of Tigris river known as *Shatt al-Arab* in Iraq and shortened to *Shatt* in the West) to Iranian vessels, unless they would sail under the Iraqi flag. With the government in Tehran insisting on the border running along the tawleg line of the *Shatt*, Iran considered this an invasion and the military was ordered to prepare for an appropriate response. A plan was set in motion, including the deployment of the merchant ship SS *Ebne-Sina* loaded with Iranian marines down the waterway, escorted by quartets of F-86s and F-5s. Further to the rear, all F-5A/Bs from the 203rd and 204th TFSs were armed with bombs and LAU-3 launchers for unguided rockets, as were 12 F-4Ds at Mehrabad, while RF-5As from the 101st TRS flew reconnaissance missions over Iraq. This massive operation served its purpose,

3-436 (c/n: N6204) was one of 14 F-5As and a single F-5B of TFB.3 deployed to Sharjah on 31 March 1967. This F-5A crashed in 1970. (Babak Taghvaee Collection)

3-422 (c/n: N.6128) one of TFB.3 F-5s sent abroad to Sharjah on 31 March 1967. This F-5A was later delivered to the SVAF in 1972. (Babak Taghvaee Collection)

Above: 3-438 (c/n: N8031) and 14 F-5As of 31st TFS were sent to Sharjah during an exercise in 1967. The aircraft in the background is 3-419 (c/n: N6124) which belonged to the 301st TFS. 3-419 had the TFB.3 badge on its vertical fin. (Babak Taghvaee Collection)

Right: 1st Lieutenant Sadeghi (right) is seen talking with his leader just minutes after his emergency landing at Vahdati AB. (Babak Taghvaee Collection)

the ship passed down the Shatt al-Arab without any kind of Iraqi interference, and the waterway was subsequently declared safe for Iranian traffic. Nevertheless, the F-5s from the TFB.2 continued flying CAPs along the Iraqi border for the next six years.

Baghdad had failed to realize its claims on the *Shatt* because Iran had now became the dominant military power in the Middle East. The IIAF – operating no less than 125 F-5A/Bs, 13 RF-5As, 30 F-4Ds, 32 F-4Es and 4 RF-4Es organized into 15 squadrons deployed at six major air bases – was the most powerful air force between Turkey and India. Although acquiring hundreds of new aircraft from the USSR, the IrAF was simply no match.

The power of the IIAF became obvious during the next crisis, which erupted in 1972, when a movement of Salafi Islamists and separatists – reportedly supported by the Afghan government – re-emerged in the Baluchistan province which is situated between Iran and Pakistan. The Pakistani armed forces reacted first, deploying ground troops to fight the insurgents. Before long they were provided air support by F-5As from the TFB.2, forward deployed to Zahedan

Captain Houshang Nahid and 2nd Lieutenant Parviz Riahi force-landed their F-5As on a road near Mashhad due to bad weather and low visibility at Mashhad airport on 14 March 1969. (Babak Taghvaee Collection)

airport that flew a number of CAS sorties. Sadly, most details about these remain unknown.

DOMESTIC MAINTENANCE SUPPORT

While negotiating the purchase of F-5A/Bs, the Iranians already understood the necessity to increase the level of proficiency of their ground personnel and develop a wide infrastructure capable of supporting modern combat aircraft.

Before 1965, IIAF technicians were trained by Iranian instructors in Iran. Their training system was out of date and unsuitable, resulting in a surplus of highly skilled aircraft sheet metal technicians, but lack of technicians specialized in hydraulics and avionics maintenance.

As such, the IIAF decided to expand and modernize its Aircraft Maintenance School in 1964. Initially the new training programme was run with inadequate facilities, insufficient training aids and devices and minimally qualified instructors. It was mostly theory, paper-and-pencil training and little practical experience. Upon graduation most of them required extensive on-the-job training resulting in few ground personnel able to undergo conversion training on the new F-5A/Bs.

This problem was identified by members of the US Military Advisory Assistance Group (MAAG) in Iran. They initiated an effort to reorganize the IIAF's Aircraft Maintenance Training Branch. A series of 18 courses were administered – usually lasting two years – to provide 408 future technicians with between 70 and 80 percent of the necessary specialized training. Emphasiss was placed on practical training and special tools and even provided for some crosstraining. Highly experienced technicians were sent for further training in the USA to qualify as instructors. The result of this process was not only that the IIAF became self-suficient in operating and maintaining its F-5 fleet – and could manage the periodic 200-hour, 400-hour and 1,200-hour checks, as well as organization-level maintenance and field-level maintenance at home – but that by the late 1960s it actually had more technicians than necessary.[*]

Furthermore, the IIAF financed the establishment and construction of the Iranian Aircraft Industries (IACI). Its Plant No. 1 at Mehrabad, undertaken with help from Lockheed and Northrop, was officially inaugurated in December 1970. Subsequently this IACI plant became responsible for depot-level maintenance of F-5s, while Plant No. 2 – situated south of Mehrabad and again constructed with help from Lockheed and Northrop, and this time also from General Electric – took over the responsibility for maintenance of General Electric J-85GE-13 turbojets that powered the Freedom Fighters.

This photo shows pilots of 43rd TTS (formerly 203rd TTS) in 1971. At the time, all of the remaining F-86Fs of Vahdati AB had been retired and these pilots were passing their transition flight training course on F-5s in the 43rd TTS at Vahdai. From left: Major Anwar (commander of 43rd TTS) and Captain Farhadi (instructor pilot). Seated from right: Lieutenant Hossein Maleki (former 202nd TFS F-86 squadron commander), Captain Talebdust, Lieutenant Ahmad Bassiriyan, Yazdan-shenas, Hooshyar, Keyvan Nourhaghighi and Shahram Rostami. (via Keyvan Noorhaghighi)

---

* This was relatively easy as the F-5 proved simple and cheap to maintain. Material costs were about US$45 per flying hour, compared to the more than US$100 per flying hour for the older F-84s and F-86s.

ENTER THE TIGER II

Despite the overall success of the introduction into service of F-5A/Bs, the Iranian government did not believe that either the F-5A/Bs or the 32 F-4Ds ordered in 1968 had improved the country's security to the degree that was necessary. Unsurprisingly, in July 1968, Tehran entered negotiations for a possible replacement, expressing interest in Northrop's next design, still in its infancy, project P.530 Cobra. A further development of the F-5, the P.530 was envisaged as a more powerful aircraft, nearly as capable as the F-4, yet a lot cheaper and simpler to maintain and operate. Anxious to acquire Northrop's new product, comprehend the technical know-how and become involved in related decision-making in Washington, the Shah went as far as expressing his interest in becoming a member of the Northrop Corporation. Related negotiations were continued through 1969 without firm results; while the Iranians insisted on replacing their F-5s with more capable aircraft during the 1970s. The Americans – neck-deep in the Vietnam War and global tensions with the USSR – proved reculant to deliver high technology to Iran.

Several independent factors changed this situation. The end of the bombing campaign in North Vietnam and general US military disengagement from South East Asia, which resulted in massive US defence savings; The British withdrawal from all its possessions east of the Suez was announced for 1971; Northrop's proposal to deliver its F-5-21 variant to Iran; Moscow's offer to deliver MiG-21MFs at the sale price of $800,000 per aircraft; and an offer from French company Dassault for Mirage IIIE fighter bombers, at a cost of $1.3 million per aircraft.

Suddenly the US defence sector became very open to orders from Iran, and thus Washington granted permission for Tehran to order enough Phantom IIs of an advanced variant F-4E to equip four squadrons in 1970. At that time the development of the P.530 was experiencing delays (partially influenced by the lack of interest from the US military for that type), thus the Iranian government – not keen on establising closer links with Moscow or enter into cooperation with Paris, which at the time was considered to have a pro-Arab stance –decided to focus on the the the F-5-21, which was later re-designated as the F-5E Tiger II. The corresponding arrangements were reached immediately after the final British withdrawal from the Persian Gulf in December 1971, when Tehran placed a firm order for 36 F-5Es, with an option for 108 more, prompting the launch of Project Peace Rush I.

In 1972 the IIAF still had not received its F-5Es, forcing F-86F pilots of the Golden Crown aerobatic display team to fly on 41st TFS F-5As for a short while. This photo was taken before one of their displays in October 1972. Sitting from left: Masoudi, Payami, Kimiyagar (leader), Aghasi-Beik and Khalili. The pilot standing is Imanian. (Babak Taghvaee Collection)

Taje Talaee (Golden Crown) aerobatic display team F-5As during an Iranian Air Force day parade in October 1972. (Babak Taghvaee Collection).

FREEDOM FIGHTERS FOR SALE

As soon as Iran had selected the F-5-21 as the replacement for the F-5A/Bs, the Iranian government was approached by Washington with requests for the resale of its Freedom Fighters to other countries, foremost to South Vietnam. The first corresponding contact between Washington and Tehran took place on 21 October 1972 when the Nixon administration asked the Shah for delivery of 90 F-5A/Bs to Saigon. The Shah was only ready to release 32 aircraft and this on condition of receiving suitable replacements. Washington persisted and the related series of meetings and message exchanges went on into November, until the USA agreed to speed up the delivery of F-5Es, to increase the total number of aircraft to be delivered and to increase the number of Iranian cadet pilots for that type to six in each training course.

Still preoccupied by its recent confrontation with Iraq, and keeping the resultant disruption of IIAF pilot training in mind, the Shah eventually agreed to deliver the requested 32 aircraft on 31 October 1972. Thus began Operation Enhance Plus. All the F-5s in question were taken from TFB.2. US technicians arrived to disassemble them and pack them onboard USAF Lockheed C-5A Galaxy transports, starting on 2 November 1972. After the US agreed to deliver the F-5Es in August 1973 and promised the inclusion of AGM-65 Maverick air-to-ground guided missiles did the Shah release two additional F-5As and nine F-5Bs for South Vietnam. The Iranian government billed Washington US$362,500 for each of aircraft bound for South East Asia – a total of US$11.6 million. At first the USAF offered three F-4Es in return, but eventually an agreement was reached that the former IIAF Freedom Fighters would be retuned to Iran as soon as the war in South Vietnam ended.

Even before Operation Enhance Plus was launched the US government requested the Iranian government to resell 21 F-5As, 11 F-5Bs and 12 RF-5As to Yemen. Lacking replacements, Tehran turned this request down. In 1974, a similar request reached Iran, though this time relating to Jordan. Maintaining good relations with

King Hussein, the Iranian government agreed with the US intention to modernize the RJAF and promised to provide 20 F-5As and two F-5Bs, including related spare engines and parts to Amman by 1975. With US promises of early F-5E deliveries in Iran's pocket, the IIAF was ready to start a planned phasing out of the remaining F-5A/Bs. The first two former IIAF F-5Bs had already been handed over to the RJAF at Mehrabad AB in March 1974. Morteza Khani recalled the first transfer flight:

At the first; Jordanian pilots were tasked to receive and transfer F-5As from Dezful, but during their first ferry flight to Prince Hassan AB in Jordan, three pilots have lost their way and were forced to make emergency landings in Saudi Arabia. Subsequently, a decision was taken to make all the remaining transfer flights by Iranian pilots – witout any problem ... Our planes carried three drop tanks for

Former IIAF F-5A with 69190 serial number is seen in SVAF service. This 42nd TFS F-5A was delivered to South Vietnam in December 1972. (via Tom Cooper Archive)

This F-5A is seen at Bien Hoa AB in South Vietnam just minutes after its arrival from Iran. Before its relocation USAF technicians had written the serial number on the vertical stabilizer. Before delivery to the SVAF on 6 November 1972, it was in service with the 41st TFS with serial number 3-401 (c/n: N6020). (via Tom Cooper Archive)

such missions, and we flew at 37,000ft (to decrease our fuel consumption to minimum) via Kuwait and Saudi Arabia straight to Prince Hassan AB.*

Ten additional F-5As and three F-5Bs were delivered by 22 May 1975. Several months before the delivery of the third batch of F-5s to Jordan, the US government asked the Iranian government to sell 10 F-5As and two F-5Bs to South Korea for US$106,000 per airframe. Intending to further reinforce the RJAF, the Shah turned this request down. The last batch of aircraft, originally destined for Jordan, arrived in June 1976, Northrop proved unable to provide additional F-5Bs to the RJAF because it had closed the production line for that variant, the Iranian government released four F-5Bs – including serials 3-7003, 3-7005, 3-7007 and 3-7012 – from the 43rd TTS, in 1978.

In Jordan, former IIAF F-5s remained in service until the mid-1980s, when 33 were re-sold to Greece, three to a US civilian company and one was used as a gateguard.

Meanwhile, many other IIAF F-5s were re-sold to other air forces. Thirty-four F-5As and seven F-5Bs went to South Vietnam, six F-5As and one F-5B to Ethiopia, and two F-5As to Morocco. Ironically, many had to be evacuated from South Vietnam after the South fell to the North in May 1975. Twelve IIAF F-5As and six F-5Bs were subsequently re-sold to South Korea, while others were returned to Iran.

PEACE RUSH I

Meanwhile, and despite the Iranian order from December 1971, the F-5-21, or F-5E, was still on the drawing board and very much still in the process of research and development. Overburdened with massive orders for F-5A/Bs from other customers, Northrop was unable to adjust its production factilities to the new type. Even one year after the initial order, the first F-5E was still years away from reaching Iran. Therefore, in December 1972, Tehran began pushing Washington to accelerate production. Facing further reductions in defence spending imposed by the US Congress, the Pentagon and the US defence sector jumped to please. Northrop accelerated its efforts and the first F-5E rolled out of the factory in Long Beach in February 1973 and the Pentagon agreed

* Khani joined the IIAF in 1970 and earned his wings during training at Lackland and San Antonio in 1973–1974. After returning to Iran he was assigned to the 43rd TTS where he qualified as an instructor pilot on F-5s.

This former IIAF F-5B with 233 s/n was one of the last F-5s sold to the RJAF. It was 3-7007 (c/n: N8064) and in service with the 43rd TTS before its delivery to the RJAF in 1978. It was later sold to a civilian user after its retirement from RJAF service in July 1990. This photo was taken in Bologna (Italy) on 25 July 1990. (via L. Alfieri via Claudio Maranta)

This rare photo taken on 21 April 1984 represents one of RJAF's No. 2 squadron F-5Bs with 226 serial number AT Mafraq AB. This ex-IIAF F-5 was sold to Hellenic Air Force. (via Ivo Sturzenegger via Claudio Maranta)

This is another former IIAF F-5A of the RJAF's No. 2 squadron with 229 serial number. This photo was taken in September 1987. (via Ivo Sturzenegger via Claudio Maranta)

The former Jordanian flag and the serial number (209) of the aircraft are seen under the faded colours of the aircraft. It was the service of the 41st TFS in IIAF with 3-491 serial number (c/n: N6446) and was then delivered to the RJAF on 22 May 1975. This photo was taken at Nea Anchialos AB in April 1996, when the aircraft was being used for gunnery training purposes. (Marinus Tabak)

This F-5B was in service with the 43rd TTS when it was procured by the RJAF in 1978. It was sold to the HAF in 1983. It was repainted and received serial number 608. (Marinus Tabak)

with combat capabilities, thus initiating Project Peace Rush III. However, with enough F-5Bs to hand, the air force was not in a particular hurry for these aircraft and they were scheduled for delivery at the end of 1977.

Overall, the IIAF intended to equip eight squadrons with 20 Tiger IIs each. In reality, they were distributed rather unevenly. The 21st, 22nd and the 23rd TFSs received a total of 54 F-5Es and six F-5Fs; the 41st and 42nd TFSs received a total of 36 F-5Es and six F-5Fs; while the 43rd TTS was issued eight F-5Fs and 10 F-5Es. The balance, 36 F-5Es and six F-5Fs, were to be assigned to the projected TFB.5, still under construction outside the town of Omidiyeh, in southwestern Iran.

The first batches of F-5Es entered service with units based at TFB.5 and TFB.6. While initially receiving serials in range 3-5xx, from 1 January 1976, they were reserialled in range from 3-7001 upward. Simultaneously, and to keep up with the pace of the construction of new facilities and the establishment of new units, the entire IIAF was reorganized. The official designation of Vahdati AFB was changed to TFB.4, while that of Tabriz was changed to TFB.2. Similarly, the 201st and 203rd TFSs were redesignated as the 41st and 43rd TFSs, while the 501st and 502nd TFSs became the 21st and 22nd TFSs. The F-5Es were used to replace F-5As within the 41st, 42nd, 21st and 61st TFSs.

The first 10 F-5Fs to arrive in Iran entered service with the 43rd TTS and the 41st TFS and were primarily used as conversion trainers. Nevertheless, they were outfitted to a far higher standard than single-seaters, including a superior TACAN/INS platform. Furthermore, because the IIAF envisaged operating them in a secondary role, that of laser-guided bombers instead of F-4Ds that were to be retired in 1980, they had all been wired to carry the AN/ALQ-101 electronic countermeasure (ECM) pods under the centreline hardpoints, and deploy GBU-10 laser-homing bombs. The Revolution of 1979 prevented the USA from delivering the necessary laser markers and other sub-systems.

that the 32 F-5Es would not be supplied to South Vietnam and Saudi Arabia, as originally envisaged, but destined for Iran instead. Under relentless Iranian pressure all 32 aircraft were completed by October that year; by then the first two IIAF pilots had completed their 75-day conversion course to that type. Deliveries to Iran commenced during the same month and proceeded at a pace of two aircraft per month, so that all 32 had arrived in Iran by October 1974, seven months ahead of schedule. As soon as the deliveries of the F-5Es to Iran began, the Iranian government placed an order for 109 more, initiating Project Peace Rush II. More than happy to please its Iranian customer, Northrop was rolling out one F-5E after another; 58 aircraft (32 from Peace Rush I and 26 from Peace Rush II) were handed over to the IIAF by the end of 1974.

Understanding the necessity for a two-seat conversion variant of the F-5E, the IIAF continued placing orders. Hard on the heels of Peace Rush I and II, it requested 28 F-5F two-seat conversion trainers

IN-COUNTRY TRAINING

Most IIAF crews had converted to their new F-5s in-country; the process proceeded smoothly, although US advisors present in Iran at that time concluded that "the best" available pilots were taken out of units in question and reassigned to projects relating to the acquisition of additional F-4s, especially the most important IIAF's acquisition of the mid-1970s: the 80 prestigious Grumman F-14A Tomcat interceptors, armed with long-range AIM-54A Phoenix AAMs.

In fact, the conversion to F-5E/Fs proceeded so smoothly that they soon became involved in joint exercises with CENTO powers and the USA. Shahbaz, 1977, saw the involvement of 22 IIAF F-4Es, 31

This is the only existing photo of the 61st TFS when it was equipped with F-5Es between 1976 and 1977. At that time 24 F-5 pilots of the squadron had the chance to experience sea-level operations. An F-5E serialled 3-7043 (c/n: U1031) is seen in the background, this aircraft was later entered on the 41st TFS inventory but was lost during an operation in the Iran-Iraq War on 30 September 1980. (Babak Taghvaee Collection)

73-0938 (c/n: U1006) is the sixth manufactured F-5E of the IIAF's Peace Rush I. It can be seen between two RoSAF F-5Es in the Northrop final assembly line in 1973. (Northrop via Tom Cooper)

F-5Es and 22 USAF F-4Es. The pilots and aircraft involved were primarily trained in air combat, including 2v1 and 2v2.[*] Colonel Samad Bala-Zadeh recalled this period as follows:[†]

After my return from the USA, me and other pilots of my training session went to the IIAF`s HQ. We were detached to Vahdati AB to pass a gunnery training course on F-5 aircraft there. I did my first flight on board of one of 43rd TTS's F-5Bs in the morning of 16th May 77 and Capt. Younes Khoshbin was my IP. After more than one month and 50 hours' flight (on-board F-5B and F-5F), I did my first solo on 23rd June 77. Two days later my formation flight training started. At the time, Vahdati AB had 8 Iranian and 2 American F-5 IPs. After around 40 days, my air combat training session was started on 5th Aug. I had three live AA shooting on TDU-10B Aerial Targeting Dart on 24th, 25th and 27th October. Gunnery training session was last part of my training by means of SUU-20 training pods, which was completed by a live Cannon and rocket firing, shooting as well as bombing on 10th Oct. After that our advanced F-5 flight and gunnery training course was ended and we graduated during a graduation ceremony on 12th Oct in the air base. Finally, after my training course, I was detached to 2nd TFB and joined 21st TFS there...[‡]

---

[*] 2v1 engagement in air combat manoeuvres (ACM), air combat tactics (ACT), and basic fighter maneuvers (BFM) is referred to engagement of two friendly fighters with an aggressor fighter, while 2v2 is for engagement of two friends with two enemies. Here Samad Bala-Zadeh is in one of two F-5Es, which had engaged with one F-4E and then two F-4Es.

[†] Quotes from Iranian pilots are presented verbatim.

[‡] Bala-Zadeh joined the IIAF in 1972, completed his basic training course the following year and advanced flight training in the USA in 1975. He returned to Iran in May 1976 and was assigned to the 41st TFS. Two years later, he was reassigned to the 21st TFS, by which time he had accumulated a total of 1,356 hours in 850 sorties. He went on to fly 121 combat sorties during the Iraqi War, and finally retired in December 1995.

Such photos are evocative for most retired F-5 pilots. This photo was taken on the apron of TFB.4 on a busy day for the personnel of the 42nd TFS in 1978. In those days, Vahdati AB averaged 90 sorties per day the combat readiness of its pilots at the highest possible level at all times. Pilots standing from right: Asil Adab (Martyr), Asghar Sedri Nowshad (Martyr), Ali Najafi, Chatrsimab, and sitting from right: Reza Zamani-Poor, Yousef Samandarian, Hamid Najafi.
(Babak Taghvaee Collection)

Memorable photo of 43rd TTS student and instructor pilots, taken in October 1976. Some of the names known are Javid Delanvar, Buick Tavakoli, Alireza Mansourian, Jahan-Bakhsh Mansouri, M.Naderi, Hooshang Mozafari, Hamid Naderinia, H.Bastani, and Reza Ramezani. (via Mike Nezam)

As in the case of F-5A/Bs, the IIAF took great care to establish the necessary support infrastructure in Iran. First, a new maintenance complex was constructed near the southern corner of Ramp No. 6 at Mehrabad AB, capable of undertaking all sorts of overhauls on F-5s. Because the F-5Es delivered to Iran were equipped with British-made Martin Baker IRQ7A ejection seats, new support contracts were finalized within the Project Peace Log to set up the necessary support facilities, for example the training of technicians, as well as the administration of necessary spare parts. This resulted in the creation of a complex computer-supported Automatic Logistic System Network that connected the IIAF HQ with all depots and bases and was designed – and proved capable – to provide spares within narrow timeframes.

IIAF F-5s were sent the IACI (Iranian Aircraft Industries) facility for heavy depot maintenance before the revolution. This photo was taken in either 1976 or 1977 and an F-5E can be seen on the IACI's apron behind the C-130 hangar. (IACI's Graphic Office)

Prince Reza Pahlavi II was a highly skilled pilot like his father. The patriotic Pahlavi family, especially Reza Shah, Mohammad Reza Shah and Prince Reza dedicated several years of their life to serving in the Iranian armed forces. Prince Reza became an F-5 pilot and started his career as a fighter pilot in IIAF. This photo was taken after his participation in the 21st Azar (12 December) parade of 1977. He is hugging Mohammad Reza Shah Pahlavi, king of Iran, and Quin Farah Diba, his mother, is watching in the background.
(Babak Taghvaee Collection)

This photo shows detachment of the 22nd TFS during its mission at Chah-Bahar in 1977. The squadron commander was Major Amir Farhadi. (www.iiaf.net)

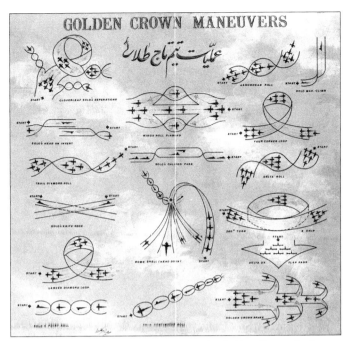

IIAF published an instruction sheet about the Golden Crown display team maneuvers in 1977. (Babak Taghvaee Collection)

FORWARD DEPLOYMENTS

The continuous instability in Baluchistan Province continued causing worries in Tehran. The IIAF was regularly deploying its fighters to Zahedan and these continued flying CAS missions in support of the Pakistani armed forces. Eventually, the situation prompted the Iranian government to consider a major expansion of military facilities in this part of Iran too.

Early in 1972, Tehran had asked the US to determine the feasibility of a naval base and air facilities at Chah-Bahar on the coast of the Gulf of Oman. In response the US Joint Chiefs of Staff sent experts to Iran to inspect the situation. The resulting study showed that a naval base with full support facilities could be constructed in the area, but that the necessary equipment and installations would cost about $77 million. Furthermore, the Americans recommended the naval facility to be protected by an air base, Hawk SAM sites, and Westinghouse ADS-4 early warning troposcatter radars, worth additional $95 million, plus facilities for an armoured brigade worth about $48 million. Undaunted, the Iranians placed a corresponding order, demanding all these facilities to completed by 1977. It was in this fashion that the TFB.10 Konarak near Chah Bahar came into being.

Although an already massive construction project, the TFB.10 was not to be left alone. In 1975 and 1976, decisions were taken to construct further bases, including the TFB.11 near Iran-Shahr, and TFB.12 near Brijand. At that time, it was expected that in this fashion the IIAF would have three major bases in eastern and southeastern Iran, and this prompted the question of how to equip the locally deployed units. That is what prompted the initiation of an Iranian search for another new type of lightweight fighter, which culminated in the IIAF's order for 140 General Dynamics F-16A/B Fighting Falcons within Project Peace Zebra, in 1977.

Meanwhile, following exercises *Shahbaz* and Mid-Link in 1977, Iranian Joint Chiefs of Staff ran the Exercise *Tajan* to test the IIAF's capabililty of repelling an invasion from Pakistan. This and another exercise in July 1978 and saw re-deployments of F-4Es, F-5E/Fs and RF-4Es to Chah Bahar, although the latter factility was still under construction. By that time the IIAF planned to gradually withdraw its F-5s from service and replace them with additional F-14s and F-16s –

Golden Crown team pilots in Shiraz airport in November 1977 just after their show. (via Tom Cooper collection)

and 215 McDonnell Douglas F/A-18A/Bs – envisaged for the period 1983-1992.

According to the IIAF's deputy of operations it had a total of 128 F-5Es and 26 F-5Fs operated by five TFSs and one TTS as of January 1979.[*] There were 11 F-5Bs (mostly returnees from South Vietnam) used for advanced training with the 43rd TTS and 11 RF-5As were still operational with the 11th TRS. Seven F-5Es were operated by the Golden Crown team. No less than 36 F-5Es and six F-5Fs, destined for the still-under construction TFB.5, were held at TFB.4.

---

[*] The IIAF is known to have lost 17 F-5As, one F-5B and six F-5Es in training accidents. One RF-5A was shot down over the USSR in the course of a reconnaissance sortie in the early 1970s and one F-5F – an example from the 21st TFS, flown by pilots Nosrat-Allah Dehkharghani and Ali Tabrizi – was shot down over the USSR by a SAM in 1977 (the latter crew lost orientation in bad weather and found themselves in Soviet airspace). Another F-5F was badly damaged in a landing accident and was undergoing extensive repairs. Overall, the relatively high number of accidents with F-5s – mostly caused through pilot error – in 1975 and 1976, prompted the air force to completely reorganize its Department of Inspection and Safety, in turn improving the overall safety of operations by a wide margin.

Left: Mohammad Reza Shah Pahlavi commending the Golden Crown's pilots after their aerobatic display at Shiraz in November 1977. (Babak Taghvaee Collection)

Below: This memorable photo of the last golden days of the IIAF shows Mohammad Reza Shah Pahlavi with the Golden Crown pilots after their formidable show to the Persian Gulf state kings and authorities in November 1977. (Babak Taghvaee Collection)

Bottom: The last pilots of the Golden Crown display team just several weeks before the withdrawal of the Pahlavi government and dissolution of the team at TFB.2 in 1979. From left: Khalili (team leader), Bolghand, Deh'kharghani, Kakwan, Golparvar, Zarifkhadem and Mostofi. (www.facebook.com/iiaf)

Chapter two
AT WAR

The series of riots that erupted in Tabriz in 1977 eventualy spread across the entire country and by late 1978 a wave of mass protests reached Tehran. While originally initiated by diverse movements, including leftists and religious sects, it culminated in what turned into an Islamic revolution that forced the Shah into exile and brought Ayatalloah Ruhollah Khomeni to power. Within two days of his arrival in Tehran, Khomeini ordered the execution of 26 generals of the Iranian armed forces. During the weekds that followed he established the Islamic Republic of Iran (IRI), with himself at the helm.

Of primary concern to the new government, was the fear of a possible coup launched from within the military, which was dominated by patriots and non-religious personnel. This resulted in a series of purges, often supported by lower-ranking officers and non-commissioned officers (NCOs, better known as *Homafars* in Iran). More than 404 officers of the Iranian military were sentenced to death by the end of 1979, and more than 60 percent of the 171,000 members of the former Imperial Iranian Armed Services were forced into early retirement, expelled, or arrested by June 1980. Finding even this unsatisfactory, the new government went on to force another 10,000 officers and NCOs to leave the service between June and October 1980.

The F-5 units went through a similar process of purges too. For example, TFB.2 came under de-facto control of rioting NCOs, who armed themselves and refused to let more than half the local officers and pilots enter the base for days. One of former members of the Golden Crown team reacalled:

'Homafars visited Khomeini and promised him their support... On 12 February 1979 a mix of Socialists and Islamists then occupied the Tabriz AB. I attempted to go to work on the morning of the next day, but one of religious sergeants, who served with the Military Police, stopped me and wouldn't let me and other pilots in. When I asked for reason, he pointed his gun on my forehead and said, 'You are one of Shah's dogs and if you ask any further questions, I will kill you. We were fired by ordinary soldiers: our retirement forms came per post already the next week.'

One of few pilots from the TFB.2 that was not 'fired', recalled the situation as follows:

I joined the air force mere months before the revolution, and only to see much disorder at TRB.2. Most of officers with the rank of Major or higher were charged by newly-invented Islamic courts, run by a lieutenant and a sergeant that were very religious, plus some fanatic Mullahs. This court later

This photo was taken during a party of TFB.2 pilots just weeks before the revolution. These pilots could not know what was about to happen to their country in the coming months; especially not how defenceless it would find itself in face of the Iraqi invasion. Indeed, Major Kamran (facing camera), was killed during the chaos following the revolution. (www.facebook.com/iiaf)

Seen here are several 21st TFS pilots and their families in Tabriz, October 1978. After the Islamic revolution of 1979, low-ranking officers and NCOs with grudges to bear took vengeance on some of the senior pilots. IRIAF bases were full of discord and animosity. Several months after this photo was taken, revolutionaries headed by Islamists and Mujahedin Khalg purged some of these pilots because of their loyalty to the Pahlavi government. (Babak Taghvaee Collection)

became the office of the Islamic Information and Guidance at our air base. Colonel Fakkouri, who flying F-4s at Mehrabad, was subsequently appointed the CO of TFB.2.

Disorder prevailed for most of 1979 and 1980. Nobody cared to maintain our aircraft, safety and discipline decreased to bellow acceptable levels, and all flying training stopped. Out of 140 pilots at TFB.2, 80 were forced to leave the service. Only 10 pilots that received permission of that 'Office' were let to fly...

Overall, the TFB.2 clocked mere six flights a week on average between February and September 1980 (compared to more than 100 sorties a day or 700 a week before the revolution). The situation at the TFB.4 was similar: the 43rd TTS was disbanded and all of its aircraft handed over to the 41st and the 42nd TFS, but these barely ever flew. Remaining F-5Bs were transferred to Mehrabad AB for storage.

BACK TO ACTION

The only air force unit that remained active for much of 1979 was the 11th TRS, still equipped with RF-5As. The reason was an armed uprising in the provinces of Kurdistan and Azerbaijan which shocked the new government. Tehran reacted with the intervention of the Islamic Revolutionary Guards Corps (IRGC), but this proved hopelessly inept in bringing the situation under control, and therefore the regular military was suddenly in demand again. In an effort to find out what was going on at ground level, the authorities needed reconnaissance pictures. This was followed by a series of uncoordinated and ineffective operations against various armed militias, primarily launched by F-4Es from TFB.3. On the contrary, F-5Es from TFB.2 did not fly any combat sorties, although much closer to the theatre of operations. The situation at these two air bases deteriorated to the point where they could not respond to a quick-reaction alert any more. Only a few F-5 pilots were sent to serve as ground observers in the west of Azerbaijan Province.

As could be expected, officers at other bases began plotting a coup against the new government. However, disorganization and an apparent warning from Soviet intelligence prevented this so-called *Nojeh* Plot. Over 50 officers from TFB.3 were arrested and – together with many from other branches of the military – were sentenced to death. At least as damaging was the fate of the 92nd Armoured Division, which lost more than 1,400 officers to arrest, forced retirement and other sorts of purges.

The obvious chaos and near disbandment of the Iranian armed services was monitored with great interest by the government of Iraq, eventually prompting it to consider an invasion of the oil-rich Khuzestan Province. To test the Iranian reaction, the Iraqis launched probing attacks against various Iranian border posts and Gendarmerie bases in April 1980. When Iranian authorities failed to react in a customary manner, the Iraqis grew bolder and in June ordered an attack of IrAF Su-20 fighter-bombers on bases of pro-Tehran Kurds inside Iran. It was only then that the TFB.4 was put on 3-Alef alert and began launching visual reconnaissance sorties along the border. The information obtained spoke directly to the degree of disarray and the obvious failure of any chain of command. One of the involved F-5Es – flown by Captain Gholam-Hoessein Bastani – was shot down by Iraqi SAMs near Shalmacheh on 25 June 1980. Additional sorties were flown by RF-4Es and RF-5As of the 11th TRS, but they did little to slow the IrAF – and helicopters of the Iraqi Army Aviation Corps (IrAAC) from frequently violating Iranian airspace and attacking border posts. The IRIAF was simply not in a condition to stop such provocations. One incident where it did took place on 25 August 1980 when two F-5Es – flown by 1st Lieutenant Mohammad-Taghi Jadidi and 1st Lieutenantt Samad Ebrahimi – used their cannons to damage an Iraqi Antonov An-2 biplane – spraying farms and oilfields inside the Iranian border with flammable liquids

This photo of the 23rd TFS pilots was taken just a few weeks before the Iraqi invasion of Iran which was launched on 22 September 1980. Nearly half these pilots were killed in the war. (Babak Taghvaee Collection)

Above: This unique photo of 2-7211 was taken by KS-92 cameras of a second RF-5A over paddies of the Caspian Sea's shores in the final years of the RF-5A's service with the 11th TRS in 1984. This aircraft played an important role during the first days of the Iran-Iraq War. (Babak Taghvaee Collection)

2nd Lieutenant Hossein Lashgari (left) and Captain Gholam-Hossein Bastani (right). During the 6,410 days Lashgari spent in Iraq prisons his family didn't know he was alive. Lashgari was tortured by the Iraqis in an effort to get him to confess that Iran had been the aggressor and had started the war, thus givinging Saddam's regime the opportunity to stop paying Iran compensation for the invasion. He was released in 1998 and died of heart attack ten years later. (Babak Taghvaee Collection)

Captain Firooz Sheikh Hasani was one of the best TFB.4 IPs. He was killed on the air base runway when Iraqi bombers scored a direct hit on his car. (Babak Taghvaee Collection)

Captain Mohammad Zare Nemati of the IRIAF. His aircraft (3-7045) was shot down over Fakkeh during his CAS mission on 18 September 1980. His family travelled to Iraq and IrAF personnel helped them try and find the body. For years both Iranian and Iraqi investigation teams searched the area but his body was never recovered. (Babak Taghvaee and Tom Cooper archives)

– forcing it to land. The crew was arrested.

Following similar incidents, what was left of the joint chiefs of staff of the Iranian armed forces finally ordered the IRIAF to halt the Iraqi aerial attacks, on 30 August 1980. Correspondingly, TFB.2 and TFB.4 were ordered to increase the readiness of their remaining pilots and again intensify their training activities. Either base was authorized to conduct up to 15 air-combat manoeuvring, gunnery and navigation flights a day.

This measure was too late; the Iraqi military was already in full swing, preparing the invasion. On 1 September its artillery shelled Qassr-e-Shirin, prompting the TFB.4 to launch a number of border patrols over the next few days, but the state of this base was so appalling that the high command of the IRIAF felt prompted to order 10 pilots and their aircraft from TFB.2 to Vahdati, in an attempt to improve the situation.

By 8 September, tensions along the border reached a point where TFB.2 was ordered to launch F-5Es from the 21st TFS to join attacks by F-4Es from TFB.3 on Iraqi ground forces. The IrAF exploited this and set up an ambush; on the following day its MiG-21MFs shot down an Iranian Phantom near Qassr-e-Shirin. On 10 December, the command post in Kermanshah requested that TFB.4 attack the al-Shohada border post in Iraq. Two F-5s executed a successful attack, but this only provoked the Iraqis into an attack on the Saleh Abad signals intelligence (SIGINT) post in Iran and the Nakhjir radio station. Eventually, the Iranians were left with no alternative but to bomb the SIGINT station themselves to destroy sensitive equipment; this was carried out by two F-5Es.

During the following days the Iraqis continued occupying one Iranian border post after the other. With the army unable to deploy more than a few mechanized companies along the border, the IRIAF continued reacting slowly, primarily sending pairs of F-5Es – one was usually armed with four Mk.82s and the other with LAU-3 rocket launchers – protected by F-14s from TFB.8 near Esfahan, into local counter-attacks. It was during one of these sorties that the Tiger II piloted by 2nd Lieutenant Hossein Lashgari was hit by Iraqi Army ZU-23 flak. The pilot was forced to eject over Iraqi positions and was captured. Lashgari was held prisoner for 18 years, supposedly as "evidence of Iranian aggression on Iraq".

On 18 September, the IRIAF pilot Captain Mohammad Zare-Nemati was killed when the F-5E 3-7045 he was flying was shot down by an Iraqi SA-6 SAM over Fakkeh.

IRAQI INVASION

On Monday 22 September 1980, at 1400, bombers and fighter bombers of the Iraqi Air Force attacked eight IRIAF bases, one civilian airport and one base of the Islamic Republic of Iran Army Aviation (IRIAA), opening Operation Glorious *Qadissiya* – Invasion of Iran.

On that day there were 70 F-5Es and 14 F-5Fs stationed at TFB.2. Five F-5Es and three F-5Fs were conducting their 1,200-hour inspections inside the maintenance hangar. Only four F-5Es – each armed with a pair of AIM-9J Sidewinder missiles – were on quick-reaction alert (QRA). Pilots were in their briefing room preparing to fly air combat manoeuvring (ACM) sorties and CAPs along the border.

The Iraqi attack hit TFB.2 at around 1345, causing minor damage to the main runway; no F-5s parked in the open came under attack. Two QRA F-5Es were launched five minutes later, but their pilots could not engage with the rapidly disappearing enemy. Both

performed emergency landings some 20 minutes later due to foreign-object damage (FOD) caused by dust and shells strewn over the runway. Tabriz air base therefore remained operational despite the Iraqis achieving complete surprise, and launched six CAP sorties by sundown.

TFB.4 was in a slightly higher state of readiness when the attack came. Four F-5Es armed with AIM-9Js and six pilots were on alert because some gunnery training sorties were planned for later that day. Seventy-seven aircraft were present at TFB.4 on that morning. Eight were not operational, ready for maintenance and eleven were not operational, ready for supply. Contrary to what most Iraqi sources claime, TFB.4 was not "only" attacked by SS-1c Scud-B surface-to-surface missiles. No Iranian sources recall any such attack. Actually, Vahdati was hit by three MiG-23s and two Su-22s at around 1330; these hits destroyed three out the 26 F-5s parked outside and the MIM-23B I-Hawk SAM site nearby, killing 18 airmen.

The second Iraqi wave came at around 1420 and hit the runway just as it was being inspected by Captain Firooz Sheikh-Hasani, deputy for safety inspection of the base. Sheikh-Hasani was killed by a bomb that landed near his car. Nevertheless, both runways were quickly repaired with the help of metal plates and TFB.4 was able to launch eight CAP sorties that evening.

OPERATION KAMAN-99

Before the revolution the Iranian armed forces were always at a high state of preparedness, ready to react quickly to any foreign aggression. Dozens of plans for various scenarios and operations had been developed and were stored in the command centres of all major military bases. When the Iraqis invaded the high command IRIAF activated one of these plans. During the afternoon of 22 September four F-4Es from TFB.3 and four from TFB.6 hit the Shoibiyah AB near Basra and Ali AB near al-Kut. More would follow: during that evening the high command ordered the execution of Operation Kaman-99, part of the war plan code-named Alborz, finalized by the HQ IRIAF on 18 August 1980. Within the frame of this operation TFB.2 was to launch 48 F-5E/Fs and TFB.4 was to launch 40 F-5Es to strike selected Iraqi military facilities early the following morning.

In spite of the perception that the air force was in disarray, these operations appear well-planned and well-coordinated. One important objective for the Tabriz Tiger IIs was the Firnas AB on the outskirts of Mosul in northern Iraq. IRIAF intelligence had assessed that the AB was protected by SA-2, SA-3 and SA-6 missile sites, plus over 20 AA gun emplacements. The Iranians pressed home their attack and scored multiple hits on the runway and several hardened aircraft shelters, as recalled by Ali-Asghar Saleh Ardestani, a pilot serving with the 21st TFS:

I flew as No.2 to Capt Afshin-Azar in a four-ship formation to hit Firnas AB. Balazadeh and another pilot were also in our formation flight [Balazadeh was No.3]. Two of us were tasked to attack hardened aircraft shelters while the other two were to bomb the runway.

We departed Tabriz at sunrise and flew at a very low altitude in a finger-four formation. Afshin-Azar and I bombed the hardened aircraft shelters after flying a pop-up manoeuvre and all our bombs hit their targets. However, Afshin-Azar's plane was hit immediately afterward. He collided with one of shelters and was killed.

Six F-5 pilots were killed in action during the operation and two others were captured. From left: 1st Lieutenant Gholam-Hossein Orooji (KIA), 1st Lieutenant Parviz Hatamian (captured), Captain Gholam-Hossein Afshin (KIA), Captain Mansour Nazerian (KIA), Major Touraj Yousef (KIA). (Babak Taghvaee Collection)

Also killed in action, 1st Lieutenant Moradali Jahanshahloo poses in front of 3-7077 (c/n: U1065). (Babak Taghvaee Collection)

TFB.4 flew attacks against Ali AB near al-Kut and the Ibn Talib AB (also known as Tallil in the West) near Nassiriya, but suffered a significant loss of six F-5Es and three pilots in the process. The F-5E 3-7142, flown by Captain Mansour Nazerian, 3-7128 flown by 1st Lieutenant Gholam-Hossein Orooji, and 3-7121 flown by Major Touraj Yousef were shot down by SAMs and their pilots were killed. Two other F-5s – 3-7124 flown by 1st Lieutenant Oveisi and 3-7042 flown by 1st Lieutenant Parviz Hatamian; the latter's aircraft crashed because of technical failures and the pilot ejected over Iraq to become a POW, while the circumstances of the loss of 3-7044 flown by Mohammad-Javad Vartavan were not clear. According to IRIAF intelligence assessments, both Iraqi air bases were rendered inoperable. Overall however, the high rate of losses was a matter of major concern and primarily the result of the inexperience and ineffectiveness of TFB.2 commander, Colonel Morteza Farzaneh, and TFB.4 commander, Colonel Mohammed-Reza Tabesh-Far, both of whom were unskilled political appointees.

Overall, TFB.2 flew an effective attack, but suffered heavy losses: the F-5E 3-7056 flown by Captain Gholam-Hossein Afshin-Azar was shot down by an SA-3, killing him. The F-5E 3-7082 flown by 1st Lieutenant Ali-Morad Jahanshahloo and the F-5E 3-7087 flown by 1st Lieutenant Mohammad Hodjati were shot down by a combination of flak and SAMs, with the loss of both pilots.

The IrAF again returned to strike TFB.2 on the morning of the 23rd but only caused slight damage to the runway, which was quickly repaired. The ground personnel were not disrupted while preparing 20 F-5Es for the next mission, a strike against al-Hurrya AB outside Kirkuk. The Iranian formation was in the process of launching at around noon when the Iraqi attack – including six Su-22s – struck. The Iraqis attempted to hit several of the F-5s that were rolling for take-off and shot two down. The Iranians were fortunate not to suffer any casualties. On the contrary, 1st Lieutenant Jamshid Owshal managed to hit one Sukhois with an AIM-9J missile, although his aircraft was heavily loaded with four Mk.82 bombs and the centreline drop tank.

Despite the enormity of the challenges they faced, the Iranian Tigers were back in the skies over Iraq on the morning of the 24th. TFB.2 launched four-ship F-5 formations to strike Iraqi air bases near Erbil and Kirkuk at 0600 and 1100 respectively. The second formation was intercepted by two MiG-21MFs on their return but Captain Yadollah Sharifi-Ra'ad outmanoeuvred one of Iraqis and shot him down with an AIM-9J missile while the MiG was shooting at the No.4 of his formation. Mustafa Ardestani participated in this mission and recalled:

Our four F-5Es were armed with Mk.82 bombs and I flew as No.2. Our plan was to attack Firnas with a pair of aircraft from the north, and another pair from the south. After dropping

A picture taken from an RF-5A shows a F-4E-damaged a HAS at al-Hurrya AB on 25 September 1980. The two MiG-21bis from No. 47 Squadron escaped serious damage. (Tom Cooper archive)

This photo was taken during 1st Lieutenant Poulad Davoudi's mission west of Dezful on 25 September 1980. Davoudi had his left stabilizer shot away. He managed to land at TFB.4 at almost double the normal landing speed. (Tom Cooper archive)

bombs, our formation leader Capt Zarif-Khadem ordered us to re-attack with 20mm cannons. I made a turn and sighted a lineup of Alouette III and Mi-2 helicopters parked on the northern apron. I lined up but my guns jammed and I couldn't shoot. Our No.3, Capt Farshid Eskandari was then shot down by a SAM while trying to hit the same lineup of Iraqi helicopters. He ejected safely and was captured by Iraqis.*

The IrAF returned the favour but one of its two Su-22M-2Ks attacking TFB.2 was shot down by a British-made Rapier SAM

---

* Mustafa Ardestani rose in rank to brigadier-general and served as deputy operations IRIAF. He was killed in an aircraft accident in 1995.

and its pilot was captured. A single F-5E was scrambled and tried to catch the other Sukhoi, but suffered a technical malfunction and its pilot, 2nd Lieutenant Amir Zanjani, was forced to make an emergency landing on a farm outside Ajab-Shir. The aircraft was subsequently returned to TFB.2 and repaired.

TFB.4 launched only one mission into Iraq later during the day; one of the involved F-5Es – the plane flown by 1st Lieutenant Bijan Harooni – was shot down by friendly ground fire near Dezful. The pilot lost consciousness during the ejection and was subsequently killed by local villagers who thought him an Iraqi.

OILY TARGETS

Following the early shock of the Iraqi invasion the IRIAF squared itself to halt the enemy advance into Khuzestan, especially since the 10th Iraqi Armoured Division was pushing straight toward Dezful. All the Iranian Army could retaliate with was Task Force 37 and the 2nd Armoured Battalion – a total of about a dozen M48 and M60 tanks. In an attempt to divert the IrAF from providing CAS to its advancing armour, to buy time for its fighter bombers to destroy Iraqi tanks and try to destroy the main Iraqi source of revenue, the IRIAF high command devised a plan for an offensive on the enemy oil industry. Correspondingly, the commanders of TFBs 2, 3, 4, and 6 were ordered to destroy the oil refineries of Basra, ad-Dowra, Qanaqin, Kirkuk and Mosul, four oilfields (Halfaya, Rumaillah, Basra and Qanaqin), the off-shore oil rigs of Mina al-Bakr and Khawr al-Amiyah, and K-1, K-2 and K-3 pumping stations on the pipeline to Jordan. The resulting operation – still run under the codename Kaman-99 – was launched on 25 September 1980.

The first missions of this operation were initiated by TFB.3 and TFB.6. F-5Es only became involved during the late afternoon when two F-5Es from TFB.2 were to bomb the oil refinery in Qanaqin and their pilots, Captain Kazem Zarif-Khadem and Captain Del-Anwar were intercepted by a pair of MiG-21MFs while approaching their target. Zarif-Khadem hit the side of a mountain while attempting to evade cannon fire from one of the MiGs; the pilot was killed.

On 27 September two F-5Es from the 21st TFS were ordered to attack a bridge in northwestern Iraq, as recalled by Jamshid Owshal:

This bridge was one of very few in that part of Iraq and thus very important for the enemy. We separated our formation and attacked from different sides. Upon releasing my bombs, I saw an ambulance car on the bridge, but I couldn't stop my bombs from hitting any more and I just said that I'm so sorry...

Later the same day, I was sent to attack Iranian Kurdish separatists base inside Iran, in an abandoned recreational and tourist complex on a hill above Haj Omran... Our planes were loaded with 160 unguided rockets and we spent them to destroy all of village's cottages. Then the forward observer advised us to attack another target nearby and we following his instructions, but this turned to be a trap. Seconds later my plane was hit by an SA-6 SAM, which set my tail section on fire. My F-5 remained flyable and I nursed it for 30km until reaching the border. However, while attempting to make an emergency landing, my flight controls failed and I was forced to eject.

On 28 September 1980 TFB.2 launched 21 sorties against oil facilities in the Hamam al-Fil, Kirkuk, Suleimaniya and Mosul areas, Ardestani recalled:

My target was oil storage facility outside Mosul, and I was assigned to load 1st Lieutenant Najafi-Mahyari. We received good target intelligence but lost the direction during ingress. Then I saw anti-aircraft fire from several guns protecting some large buildings. I decided to attack them instead of continuing the search for our target: my logic was that only important places would be protected by AA guns. I informed my No.2 and we flew a good attack. During our return to Iran, we found a P-14 radar site and fired all of our 20mm ammunition at it.

Similar sorties were made against targets during the following two days. All participating F-5Es carried four Mk.82s, two AIM-9Js and 140 rounds of ammunition for their internal Colt M39 20mm cannons. The IRIAF suffered only one loss: the F-5E 3-7138 was shot down over Kirkurk and its pilot, Captain Asadollah Akbari Farahani, ejected safely but was taken prisoner. Ardestani recalled this mission:

Our target on 29 September was the oil storage facility northeast of Kirkuk. I was meanwhile familiar with the area and local Iraqi air defences, and knew that this was one of most dangerous places in Iraq to go to...

During the ingress, my No.2 informed me that his external fuel tank is not feeding, but – guessing he had probably forgotten to retract his flaps – I ordered him to continue the mission. We reached Kirkuk and I saw our target. We approached at low altitude, flew our pop-up manoeuvre and delivered our ordnance on target, causing a big explosion....

Then my No.2 informed me that he had only 1,600lbs of fuel left – not enough to reach Tabriz. I ordered him to climb in order to decrease fuel consumption and watched him high above me for the rest of our flight. We recovered safely back in Tabriz.

The next day, I was to fly a similar mission against an oil storage facility outside Erbil. It was my eighth combat sortie of that war and I was to lead Captain Ghorbani.

We reached the target undisturbed: I saw a number of drilling machines and other equipment and released my bombs upon them, causing them to explode. On the way back I spent my 20mm ammo on an Iraqi military base.

With the F-5Es from TFB.4 preoccupied with fighting for the survival of their base, the pressure was on F-5-pilots from TFB.2 to continue flying such dangerous missions during October 1980

too. On the 5th of that month, 10 F-5Es bombed two targets in the Kirkurk area, flying straight into t a barrage of Iraqi cannon fire. The fin and exhaust nozzles of the F-5E 3-7079 flown by Colonel Mohammad Daneshpour were riddled with shrapnel holes, and the pilot recalled:

My plane was hit by 57mm flak while I was descending to release my Mk.82s. I felt the impact but released my bombs as planned and then escaped into a narrow valley behind the target. As next I started checking all my systems: several warning lights were on and I saw that the left engine was losing power. I turned the fuel supply to that engine off to prevent fire and asked my No.2 to inspect my aircraft and announce my emergency landing to the TFB.2.

Everything was under control: I was underway on one engine but still doing 550km/h. To avoid interception by Iraqi MiGs I frequently made turns for 30-40 degrees left of right... I reached Tabriz and called the ground control, explaining my left engine and main hydraulic system were out. I used the secondary system to drop my undercarriage and then descended to land. On finals, I activated the braking chute – only to find out there is none: my t-handle for the chute went lose and was dangling. Left without a choice, I pulled the nose of my plane up, touched down and started pressing the brakes. Even so, my plane was stopped only by the arrest barrier at the end of the runway. Iraqis later announced that I was shot down: they thought I was ejecting because their flak shot away my braking chute![*]

On 10 October, the 22nd TFS lost its commanding officer (CO), Captain Asadollah Barbari, during an attack on the Mosul oil refinery. Barbari did not manage to eject and was killed on impact. The Iraqis buried him in the military cemetery of Neinawa, but his remains were returned to Iran after the war. Also shot down during that attack was the F-5E flown by 1st Lieutenant Ibrahim Del-Hamed, who was was also killed in action.

Following a pause of several days, the IRIAF again hit the Iraqi oil industry on 26 October when four F-5Es destroyed nine giant fuel tanks at the Kirkuk refinery and a nearby pumping station on the K-pipeline. When the IRIAF realized that the Iraqis were repairing this facility, it was attacked again by two F-5Es on 3 November, again causing heavy damage. However, the F-5E flown by Captain Hamid Fazilat was shot down by a SAM over the town of Rawanduz during the egress and the pilot was killed. Additional strikes, on 8 and 14 November, saw TFB.2's F-5Es hitting Kirkuk and Mosul with Mk.82 bombs again, rendering nearly 80 percent of the local oil facilities inoperable; Iraq lost more than 900,000 barrles of oil from these strikes alone. The Iranians paid a heavy price for this success, losing the F-5E 3-7122 flown by 1st Lieutenant Parviz Zabihi Atr-Kola, who was shot down and killed. Ardestani recalled the mission from the 14th:

It was Friday and I flew my 34th combat sortie of the war. We've attacked the oil storage facilities outside Mosul often before but did not manage to completely destroy it. One of problems

---

[*] Daneshpour survived the war. He retired with the rank of brigadier-general and went on to establish the IRIAF strategic research and studies office. He died from a heart attack in the late 1990s.

F-5E pilots who lost their lives in the course of Operation Kaman-99, from left: 1st Lieutanant Bahram Ali-Moradi, 1st Lieutenant Mahmood Mohammadi Noukhandan, 1st Lieutenant Parviz Zabihi Atr-Kol, Captain Asadollah Akbari Farahani and Captain Asadollah Barbari. (Babak Taghvaee Collection)

This F-5E was damaged by 57mm flak rounds during a strike mission against Dukan Dam on 5 October 1980 while flown by Colonel Mohammad Daneshpour. The entire boat tail and rudder were later replaced and the plane was returned to service two years later. It was eventually lost during Operation Valfajr-8 on 23 February 1986. (Babak Taghvaee Collection)

the Iraqis caught Zabihi, hit his plane and killed him. I dove towards valleys on the Iraqi-Turkish border, then turned right towards Iran... By the time I reached Iran, I was so short on fuel I had to land at Orumiyeh airport instead, where Sharifi-Raad landed too.

Overall, more than half of about 40 major strikes flown against the Iraqi oil industry in the autumn of 1980 were undertaken by F-5Es, most of them by TFB.2. In general, this operation was considered highly successful; it not only caused the intended damage but effectively forced Baghdad to halt all oil exports and even curb the operations of its ground forces inside Iran. For two weeks Iraqi tanks in Khuzestan were stranded without fuel, exposing them to the full force of the IRIAF.

BATTLE FOR VAHDATI

While TFB.2 bore the brunt of operations against the Iraqi oil industry, TFB.4 fought a fierce battle for the survival of its base near Dezful and for the Khuzestan Province. The importance of the endurance and performance of the pilots and ground crews from this base cannot be over-emphasized. In the Khuzestan Province the Iranian Army was only able to pit 138 Infantry Battalion, Task Force 37, and the 2nd Armoured Brigade of the 92nd Armoured Division – reinforced by a single tank battalion from the 77th Infantry Division – against the invading force of two full corps, a total of eight divisions and several independent brigades of the Iraqi Army.

The F-5 pilots from TFB.4 had been flying CAS missions since 25 September, primarily in support of the 2nd Brigade – a formation only by designation. It had five operational M60A1 main battle tanks (MBTs) and three M113 armoured personnel carriers (APCs), facing the onslaught of the 3rd and 10th Iraqi Armoured Divisions, 1st Mechanized Infantry Division and several independent brigades.

was that we could often not find our targets. Because of this, an RF-4E flew a recce sortie over our target a day earlier, and thus we finally have got some very good photos.

Because of the importance of this mission, our formation was led by Colonel Daneshpour. I was his No.2, while Captain Yadollah Sharifi-Raad led 1st Lieutenant Zabihi as Nos. 3 and 4...

We approached our target in full radio silence flying along the border to Turkey and then towards the east, practically 'returning' in direction of Iran. I saw No. 1 and No. 3 releasing their bombs precisely on target, and followed in fashion.

Then our formation separated: while we flew north, Zabihi turned east, which was wrong. I broke radio silence and informed him about his mistake, so he rejoined. On the way back Zabihi noticed some Iraqi military outpost and dove to attack with his 20mm cannon. He was happy and thrilled and imitated his cannon's sounds on the radio while firing...

Then two MiG-23s appeared behind us. I warned everybody to jettison drop tanks and engage afterburners. It was too late,

Task Force 37 fought skilfully until surrounded by the Iraqis in the area of the crossroad between Dehloran and Ein-e-Khosh. Elsewhere, the Iraqis overran the Dehloran early warning radar site on 25 September, as well as most of the ZU-23 and Oerlikon AA guns protecting it; the captured 39 personnel from the base in the process. The F-5Es from the 41st TFS launched a series of strikes to destroy as much of captured equipment as possible, but lost one F-5 and its pilot to friendly fire.

With the crucial city of Dezful and thus the Vahdati AB under direct threat, the Iranian Joint Chiefs of Staff redirected all their available assets in this direction. This comprised an infantry battalion that was transported by C-130s and Boeing 747 transports from Tehran, a battalion of marine rangers from Bandar Abbas, an artillery group from Esfahan and the 77th Infantry Division dispatched its sole operational tank battalion. Even so, army commanders had little choice but to call the IRIAF for help. The CO TFB.4 summoned all 107 pilots under his command to a briefing. He had 77 operational F-5Es under his command (seven aircraft were lost between 22 and 29 September) and wanted to run 50–64 CAS sorties per day until the Iraqis were finally stopped. The TFB.4 command post (CP) was converted into a field headquarter for all involved branches of the military, even used by Iranian President Abolhasan Bani-Sadr and the CO of the armed forces, Brigadier-General Zahir-Nejad.

Understanding that TFB.4 would be left practically defenceless during this all-out effort, the IRIAF high command deployed one of its TPS-11 mobile tactical radars to the area, and tasked F-14As from the 81st and 82nd TFS with providing continuous top cover for the base. Furthermore, RF-4Es and RF-5As of the 11th TRS were to fly reconnaissance from TFB.1.

The counter-attack by TFB.4 was launched early on the morning of 27 September and saw F-5Es and F-5Fs flying so intensely that detailed descriptions of their operations cannot be supplied in this narrative due to their volume. In several dozen sorties, they relentlessly saturated columns of Iraqi armour with CBU-57/Bs and Hunting BL.755 cluster bomb units (CBUs) and rockets from LAU-3 launchers. Except for pre-planned sorties, on-call CAS missions were conducted as well, hitting targets anywhere between Dasht-e-Abbas, Naderi Bridge, Mussian, Dehlroran, Fakkeh, Ali Gereh-Zad Heights and toward the Allah-u-Akbar Heights. Because of the proximity of the battlefield to TFB.4, the average sortie lasted only 50 minutes.

On the first day of this operation, the F-5Es delivered a total of 166,400lbs of bombs and expended 32,000 rounds of 20mm ammunition in 64 sorties, losing one F-5E serial 3-7133 and its pilot, Major Fat'h-Allah Gholam-Rezaiee.

On 28 September, 68 sorties were launched, delivering 176,800lbs of bombs and 34,000 20mm rounds. Once again, one F-5E failed to return; Captain Hossein Moghimi was shot down and killed over Ein-e-Khosh. After suffering a loss of nearly 100 armoured vehicles to Iranian aerial strikes in the course of two days, the impact of the IRIAF operation was such that after one F-5 attack on 28 September, the 42nd Iraqi Armoured Battalion collapsed, its crews fleeing and leaving behind two dozen intact T-55 and T-62 MBTs, all of which were captured. Nevertheless, the Iraqis relaunched their advance the following day, forcing the 2nd Brigade back with only two intact M60s and two M113s. Badly battered, the Iranian army formation counterattacked, attempting to recapture the Ali Gereh-Zad Heights. This attack collapsed in the face of murderous Iraqi artillery fire, which killed even the CO of the 2nd Brigade and most of his

officers, forcing survivors to flee toward the Karoun River. Despite this success, the Iraqis did not attempt to press home the advantage; instead they buried and camouflaged their tanks for the rest of the day, hiding and waiting for the following night to push forward. Pilots from TFB.4 thus found fewer targets to attack on the 29th, and are known to have spent 60,000lbs of bombs and 10,000 20mm shells. Nevertheless, they claimed the destruction of 60 additional Iraqi vehicles.

TFB.2 TO THE RESCUE

On 29 September 1980, the IRIAF HQ ordered TFB.2 to detach eight of its best pilots and eight F-5Es to reinforce Vahdati. Mustafa Ardestani, Samad Ali Bala-Zadeh, Samad Naghdi, Hossein-Pour and four others volunteered for this task and arrived at TFB.3 the following day where the decision was taken for them to operate from that base instead of continuing to Vahdati because the latter was under such critical threat. Their Tigers were immediately refuelled, armed and dispatched into a strike in support of TFB.4. Tigers from Vahdati launched a further 30 CAS sorties, expending 30 CBU 57/Bs and BL.755s, and ten LAU-3 pods in the process. Two F-5Es failed to return: 3-7043 flown by Amr-Allah As'adi Yassaghi and an unknown aircraft flown by Captain Gholam-Hossein Khosh-Niyat. Both pilots were killed.

On 1 October 1980 the F-5Es flew 34 CAS sorties against Iraqis in northern Khuzestan, deploying 88,400lbs of bombs and 17,000 20mm rounds. Mustafa Ardestani recalled his mission on that day:

> We launched from Nojeh early in the morning, with me and 1st Lt Naghdi flying in direction of Ein-e-Khosh, some 100 kilometres inside Iran, but occupied by Iraqis. I had no experience in attacking mobile targets, but once we reached the target area we found the Iraqis entrenched and camouflaged. We released CBUs on the first pass and then attacked with cannons, then flew to Vahdati to re-fuel and re-arm. Naghdi and me volunteered to fly another mission latter that day, against Iraqis in Ali Gereh-Zad area, south of Ein-e-Khosh. We found plenty of targets there, and released our CBUs on the first run, then made a u-turn and shot at Iraqi troops running towards the Dehloran radar site with 20mm cannon.
>
> Back in Vahdati, I volunteered for my third sortie, and was joined by Hossein-Poor. We attacked an Iraqi column north of Shuh, only 30 kilometres from Dezful, shortly before the sunset, which make it hard to see their exact position. Nevertheless, we sighted several heavy machine-guns and released our CBUs directly on the top of them.

Although the intensity of operations decreased on 2 October, TFB.4 again launched 30 sorties, primarily targeting the 3rd Iraqi Armoured and 1st Mechanized Division west of Karakeh. One F-5E serial 3-7033 flown by 1st Lieutenant Bahram Ali-Moradi was shot down by Iraqi SA-6 fire from a site outside Ein-e-Khosh. Ardestani flew two sorties that day:

> Naghdi and I were tasked to attack Iraqis in the town of Shalamcheh. Our aircraft were armed with napalm bombs and our targets was a miscellany of Iraqi trucks reportedly moving in that area. Indeed, we found the zone full of potential targets,

Some of the participants in the Battle for Vahdati. Front row from left: 1st Lieutenant Hadi Jouraki (KIA), 1st Lieutenant Hossein Bahram (KIA), 1st Lieutenant Seif-Allah Sarmadi and Captain Abdol- Majid Taghavi. Top row from left: Captain Abulfazl Asad-Zadeh (KIA), Captain Ahmad Kottab (PoW), Captain Changiz Sepehr (KIA), Major Fat'h-Allah Gholam-Rezaiee (KIA). (Babak Taghvaee Collection)

Four of best 21st TFS pilots can be seen in this photo taken in 1977. From left: Ahmad Taramchi, Ata Mohebbi, Samad Balazadeh and Mohammad Ahmadzadeh. (via Kouros Pashazadeh)

and after a short search I released on the biggest one – an ammunition carrier. My bombs failed to detonate and that made me very angry... On the way back to Vahdati, I found several Iraqi tanks near the city of Khorramshar and attacked them with 20mm cannons. That day, the Iraqis occupied that city, and we were all very angry and upset!

Tigers from Vahdati flew another 28 combat sorties on 3 October, primarily against Iraqi troops close to Dezful. Nevertheless, they also flew two missions into Iraqi airspace, targeting the rear bases of the 1st Mechanized and 10th Armoured Divisions and destroying the SA-6 site near Ein-e-Khosh that shot down 1st Lieutenant Ali-Moradi. Ardestani continued:

> Capt Ra'esee that came with me from TFB.2 was forced to make an emergency landing on Dehloran highway strip, three days ago. Vahdati dispatched a team of technicians that repaired his F-5E despite several attacks by Iraqi MiG-23BNs. We flew a CAP over this area, until Ra'esee was able to take-off and then escorted him back to TFB.4.
>
> In the afternoon, Naghdi and me volunteered for another mission and attacked Iraqis near Ein-e-Khosh again. We found lots of targets and were sad that we only had a limited amount of ammunition. We bombed and then returned to Vadhati, only to learn the base came under attack of two MiG-23 in the meantime. The ground control therefore ordered us to go to TFB.3 and land there. We've spent the night in Hamedan and the next morning returned to Vahdati again.

This Battle for Khuzestan continued on 4 October when F-5Es flew 22 sorties, losing one of theirs in the process. The plane flown by Shahab-Aldin Tabatabaee-Solatni was shot down by friendly fire and the pilot was killed. Following on from earlier successes, 5 October 1980 turned into a major catastrophe for TFB.4: out of 8 F-5Es launched early in the morning, four were lost, together with two pilots. The first, F-5F 3-7178 flown by Captain Abdol-Majid Taghavi, was lost to technical manlfunction during take-off. The pilot ejected but was injured. Two F-5Es, 3-7036 flown by 1st Lieutenant

Hadi Jouraki and 3-7129 flown by Captain Changiz Sepehr, were shot down by Iraqi SA-6 fire; both pilots were killed. Finally, the F-5F 3-7156 flown by Captain Ahmad Kottab was hit by SA-6s too, as recalled by Samad-Ali Bala-Zadeh:

> The Iraqis had occupied Chanaeh and we were ordered to bomb their positions. Kottab was the leader of our formation and he ordered us to climb to 10,000ft before attacking. Recalling lessons about Iraqi SAMs Colonel Daneshpour gave us at Tabriz, I recommended approach at minimal altitude, but Kottab insisted that this was too dangerous because of flak. Eventually, we decided to fly low, but once over the target, Kottab climbed sooner than originally planned and a SAM hit his Tiger. His plane was cut in two and Kottab was forced to eject.
> Enraged, I turned in the direction from which the SAM had come, firing my rockets at the place I thought the missile was. The Iraqis fired another SA-6 at me and I had to evade, pulling plenty of Gs. The missile exploded nearby, throwing my aircraft out of control for several seconds. I levelled out, only to see the launcher with two SA-6s in front of me. I passed above, then made a u-turn and came back, blasting with my 20mm cannons all the way and ignoring two further SAMs that flashed above my F-5.

On the last day of the all-out operation in defence of TFB.4, F-5Es flew 18 sorties to drop 20 Mk.82s, 16 BLU-1B napalm bombs and 10 BL.755s, and expend 4,500 20mm rounds. These attacks finally broke the will of the Iraqi 1st Mechanized and 10th Armoured Divisions and forced them to start withdrawing west. The IRIAF lost two Tigers, including 3-7026 flown by 1st Lieutenant Seif-Allah Sarmadi, who ejected 35 kilometers north of Vahdati after both engines flamed out and was wounded on landing; and 3-7115 flown by 1st Lieutenant Hossein Bahram was shot down directly over the enemy position and killed.

Instead of three days, as expected by Iranian commanders, the Battle for Vahdati lasted 15 days.[*] While suffering heavy losses in F-5E/Fs, the IRIAF flew 324 sorties to rout two Iraqi army divisions, forcing them to withdraw after the loss of more than 170 MBTs and APCs, and hundreds of other vehicles. Finally, F-14s providing top cover usually managed to effectively seal off and deny the aerial battlefield to the IrAF, forcing the Iraqis to abort their attacks; however, they still managed to shoot down four Iraqis that insisted on entering the combat zone.

LOSSES TO MIGS

During the first week of the war, the IRIAF launched an operation with the aim of disrupting Iraqi power plants and power-supply networks. Related strikes were primarily flown by F-4Es, but F-5Es from TFB.2 became involved on 1 October and were tasked with attacks on hydroelectric facilities in northeastern Iraq, such as the Dukan Dam and Darabandikan facility. As soon as the Iraqis launched

repairs on the Dukan Dam, this was reattacked by two F-5Es on 3 October and then two F-4Es from TFB.3 the following day.

Follow-up strikes in this series of operations were undertaken on 16 November 1980, when four F-5Es from TFB.2 hit the Penjwin power plant, and then again on 21 and 26 November, eventually prompting the IrAF to deploy MiG-21MFs and MiG-21bis to fly intensive CAPs over the area. Ardestani recalled the events 21 and 26 November as follows:

> 1st Lieutenant Ra'iesse and me were ordered to hit the Dukan power plant again. That facility was one of the best-protected in entire Iraq by that time. We attacked it several times, but never managed to cause sufficient damage to knock it off. So also on 21 November, when our bombs went wrong... Five days later we attacked the place again, though this time in combination with simultaneous attacks on radar station in Halabcheh, military base in Suleimaniyah, and al-Hurrya AB outside Kirkuk. I was with the pair that attacked the radar in Halabcheh. We released our bombs precisely, but these failed to hit. Then I fired my 20mm cannons, but the radar kept working.
> Meanwhile, the two F-5Es underway to attack Suleimaniyah were intercepted by two MiG-21s and the Iraqis have shot down the plane [serial 3-7105; author's note] flown by 1st Lt Amir Zanjani. The leader of that pair, Capt Sharifi-Raad, released his bombs and then outmanoeuvred the other MiG, downing it with few hits from 20mm cannons and manoeuvre. Worse was to follow, then no sooner that we landed back at TFB.2, ground crews informed us about the death of 1st Lieutenant Abul-Hassan Abul-Hasani, shot down while attacking the Dukan Dam.

Abul-Hasani was shot down while flying the F-5E 3-7080. Sharifi-Raad recalled this mission as follows:

> It was the 65th day of the war and I went to the CP to pick up my orders... I was assigned to fly a mission originally scheduled for Capt Javadpour, one of best pilots of our base... My wingman was 1st Lt Amir Zanjani...
> Our target was an enemy observation post, but I found it empty and decided to re-route our formation towards the telecommunication facility outside Suleimaniyah instead. Once there, my plane shook and I warned my wingman about enemy flak. Then I glanced to the left and sighted a MiG-21: that was the reason for my aircraft shaking. I released my bombs and prepared for air combat while decreasing my altitude to a very low level and then turning hard to force the MiG to overshoot. The Iraqi pilot did a mistake and reduced his speed, while I did another mistake by firing an AIM-9J at him much too early. The Sidewinder failed to lock-on and missed its target.
> I switched to guns and fired a burst at his right wing from short range. He was watching me as we descended very low, and then his left wing touched the ground – and his aircraft exploded.
> I returned to Tabriz alone. Upon landing, I found out that Zanjani collided with the second MIG-21, and that both pilots were KIA. Zanjani was a true patriot, calm and polite pilot and I am never going to forget his face or his voice.

---

[*] F-5Es from the TFB.4 continued pursuing Iraqi units that were withdrawing from Dezful for four more days. In the course of one of these final missions, the F-5E flown by Jahanbakhsh Mansouri on 10 October 1980 was shot down by SA-6s between Shadegan and Ahwaz, and the pilot was killed. During the following days, two additional F-5Es were lost in the same area; these were flown by 1st Lieutenant Mohammad Vakili Zaheer and 1st Lieutenant Mohammad Mortezaiee Friz-Heindi, both of whom were killed.

This photo was taken by Captain Sharifi-Ra'ad's gun camera just before he fired at the MiG-21MF. (via Tom Cooper archive)

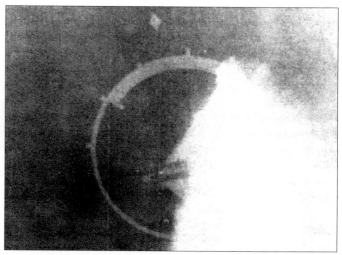

This is a gun camera picture taken by Major Javadpour during air combat on 17 October 1980. It shows an Iraqi Su-20 or Su-22 (both flew strikes on TFB.2) going up in flames. (via Tom Cooper Archive)

Ali-Asghar Saleh Ardestani participated in the attack on Dibs power plant, flown on 9 December 1980:

> I flew together with Nasrollah Erfani... We approached the target at low altitude and undisturbed, but the Iraqis sighted us when we were several kilometres away, and opened fire with anti-aircraft artillery. We dove and released our bombs on the target, then turned in opposite direction. One SA-3 was fired at my plane but didn't track because I flew too low.

Mustafa Ardestani bombed the Kirkuk power plant the same day:

> I was with the second formation, led by Col Daneshpour... We appeared over the target and Daneshpour separated from our formation to hit the power plant of the refinery located east of the city. We then bombed the refinery and its high-voltage station. Results were successful, because we caused widespread damage. Iraqi national radio later claimed 20 Iranian warplanes had attacked but that their SAM sites shot down five. Actually, we did not lose anybody that day.

The last day of this campaign was on 19 December when 12 F-5Es hit powerplants in Kirkuk, Radan, Debis and Penjwein, hitting 80 percent of their targets and causing a blackout in most of northeastern Iraq. One Tiger was shot down by SAMs and then IrAF interceptors appeared too, as recalled by Mustafa Ardestani:

> We didn't fly for nearly a week because of bad weather, but on 19 December I was assigned a mission to Debis power plant. Captain Sharifi-Raad was leader, Capt Abbassian his No.2, and Capt Baghaiee my wingman as No.4...We approached our target by flying high above the clouds then dove to bomb and hit very precisely. Afterwards we lost the sight of each other because of clouds and began calling on the raid for joining up. The Iraqis had one Antonov An-26B – nicknamed Qamar – equipped for SIGINT and that plane detected us, vectoring two MiG-23s to intercept. When we were some 70km away from the border, MiGs came from our front and crossed to our left trying to turn around and engage us from behind. I called them to Daneshpour but he told me that I am confused and there

Captain Ali Dogaheh was one of the best TFB.2 pilots. He participated in a strike mission against the Aqrah military camp in the Sulaymaniyah province. His aircraft was shot down and he ejected. The Iraqis beheaded him and sent his head to an Iraqi commander. His body was buried without its head. This horrible fact was revealed by the Iraqis after the fall of the Saddam regime. (Babak Taghvaee)

3-7154 was first IIAF F-5F tested by Northrop before delivery in 1976. The 28 F-5Fs replaced the six Zot Box-equipped F-4Ds (with LGB capacity). Each F-5 squadron had three or four F-5Fs capable of precision bombing via LGBs, with further plans in place to fit AN/ALQ-101 ECM pods for self-defence. (Tom Cooper)

3-7099 (c/n: U1087) was Major Khalili's aircraft when he served as leader of the Golden Crown aerobatic display team and later as CO TFB.2. In 1980, 3-7099 was repainted in Asia Minor II camouflage colours but crashed in the fifth year of the war. (Tom Cooper)

By 1985 most surviving RF-5As were unserviceable, with pilots flying F-5Bs on continuation training. F-5Bs saw service with the South Vietnamese air force between 1972 and 1975. The F-5B 3-7001, flown by Major Poulad Dawoodi crashed on 28 February 1985, killing Dawoodi.. (Tom Cooper)

On 6 October 1980, 3-7026 (c/n: U1014), armed with four BLU-1B napalm bombs and piloted by Lt. Seif-Allah Sarmadi, was one of several F-5Es shot down by enemy AA fire. The aircraft crashed 20 miles north of Vahdati; the pilot ejected but was badly injured. (Tom Cooper)

On 5 October 1980, 3-7036 (c/n: U1024), armed with four LAU-3A rocket launchers and piloted by Lt. Hadi Jouraki, was shot down by an SA-6 and the pilot KIA. (Tom Cooper)

3-7045 s/n (c/n: U1033) of 42nd TFS, armed with four LAU-3A rocket launchers and piloted by Capt. Mohammad Zare Nemati, was shot down by an Iraqi SA-6 on 18 September 1980. (Tom Cooper)

3-7079 was armed with four Mk.82SE retarded bombs on its final mission. It had been repainted in Asia Minor II camouflage pattern only two months earlier, as it had served as aircraft No. 5 of the Golden Crown team. (Tom Cooper)

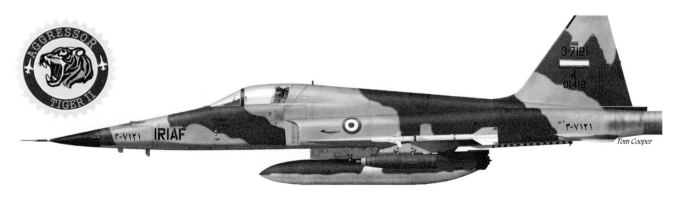

3-7121 (c/n: U1109), armed with four Mk.82SE retarded bombs and piloted by Maj. Touraj Yousef, was one of five TFB.4 F-5Es lost on 23 September 1980. Inset: the patch worn by pilots with 1,000 hours on Tiger IIs out of TFB.4. (Tom Cooper)

3-7122 (c/n: U1110) was flown by Lt. Parviz Zabihi Atr-Kola when it was shot down on 14 November 1980. Inset: the patch worn by pilots with 1,000 hours on Tiger IIs out of TFB.2. (Tom Cooper)

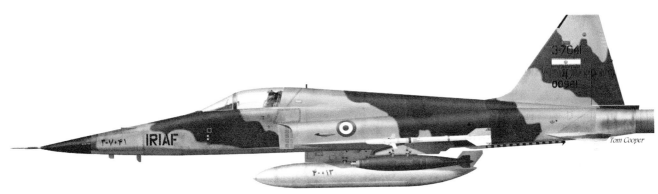

3-7041 (c/n: U1029), piloted by Lt. Mahmood Mohammadi Noukhandan, was shot down on 4 October 1980 on a mission against the Basra oil refinery. (Tom Cooper)

3-7133 (c/n: U1121), armed with four CBUs and piloted by Maj. Fat'h-Allah Gholam-Rezaiee, was shot down on 27 September 1980. The artwork shows the three principal types of cluster bombs used by Iranian F-5s, including, from left, CBU-59, CBU-57/B and the British-made Hunting BL.755. (Tom Cooper)

The RF-5A 2-7203 was the last example of this variant that served as an operational reconnaissance platform. Its old cameras were replaced with the KS-121 70mm Aerial Reconnaissance Camera System as used on the RF-5E (this variant was never operated by Iran), clandestinely acquired abroad and installed by the TFB.7 SSJD team. It wore the same livery as most Simourghs. (Tom Cooper)

The first Owj Complex F-5E Azarakhsh was painted in this fashion, firstly in the yellow zinc-chromate colour overall, and then in Iranian colours similar to those worn by the former Golden Crown team. The aircraft was subsequently repainted in Asia Minor II camouflage pattern and received the serial number 3-7301. Inset shows the little-known emblem of the Owj Complex. (Tom Cooper)

The Owj Complex 3-7364 F-5E Azaraksh was the third example of this variant. It became famous on the internet for its photoshopped image, showing it with mid-installed wings. It was later rebuilt as Saegheh 3-7369. (Tom Cooper)

Similar to other IRIAF F-5Fs, 3-7174 wore Asia Minor II camouflage colours before it was repainted in the Azarakhsh colour scheme in order to participate in the Holy Defence Week parade of 2007. The insets show a review of weapons deployed by the type during the war with Iraq and other emergencies, including, from left, LAU-3 launcher for unguided rockets, Mk.82 'slick' bomb, Mk.82SE, M-117 general-purpose bomb and Mk.84 bomb. (Tom Cooper)

The projected IAMI/Owj Complex Kowsar-88 prototype was rolled out in 2014. (Tom Cooper)

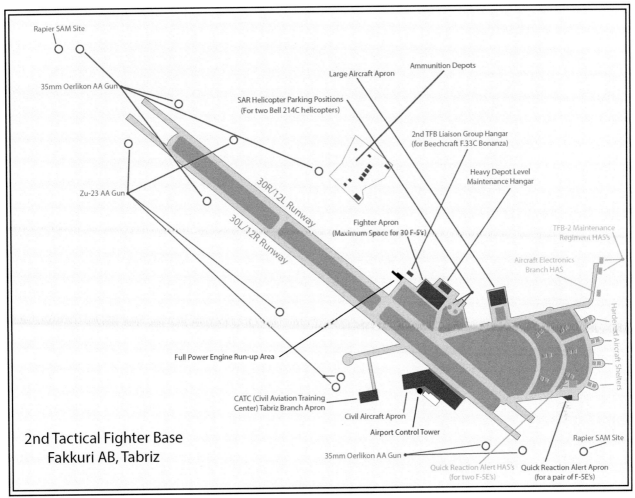

This map shows TFB.2 on 22 September 1980. (Map by George Anderson)

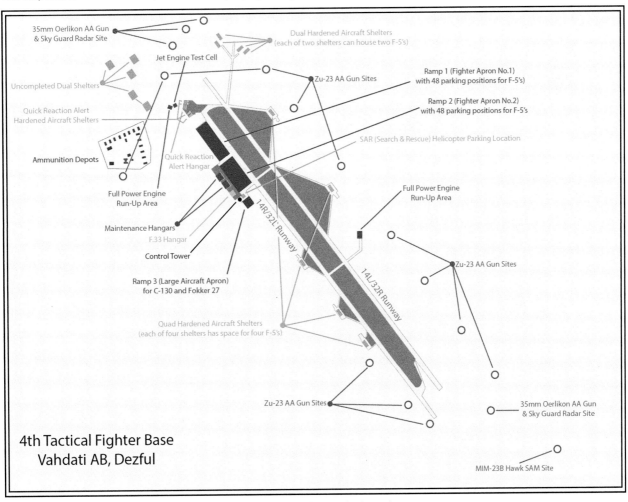

This map shows TFB.4 Vahdati on 22 September 1980. (Map by George Anderson)

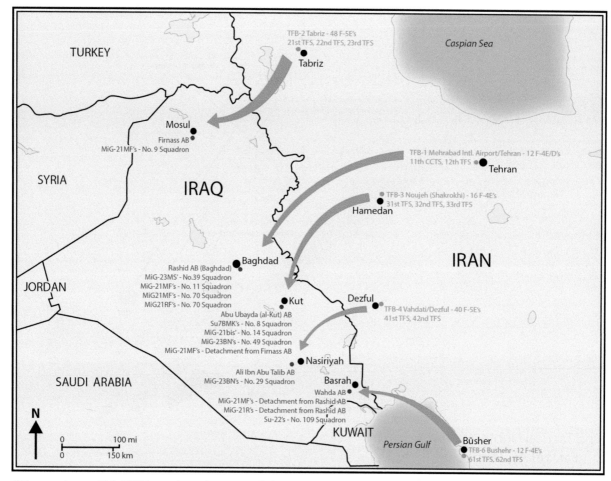

This map shows which IRIAF squadrons, how many airplanes attacked which IrAF air bases during the first phase of the operation 140-aircraft (also known as Kaman-99). The IrAF's air bases are also indicated. (Map by George Anderson)

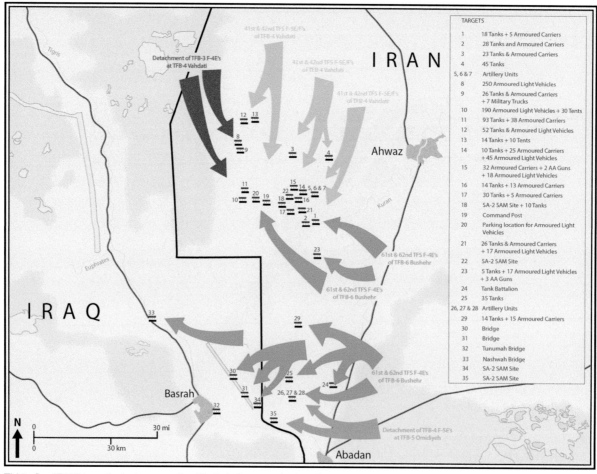

Thirty-five IRIAF targets during operation Shabah-3 are marked on the map exactly according to the frag orders of the operation. (Map by George Anderson)

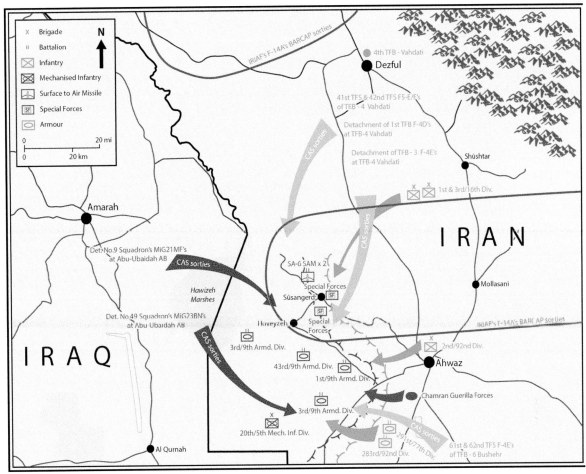

This map shows Iranian and Iraqi frontlines and positions during Operation Nasr. Iranian army aviation played a significant role in MEDEVAC and CAS missions during the operation but details of its flights are not shown on the map.
(Map by George Anderson)

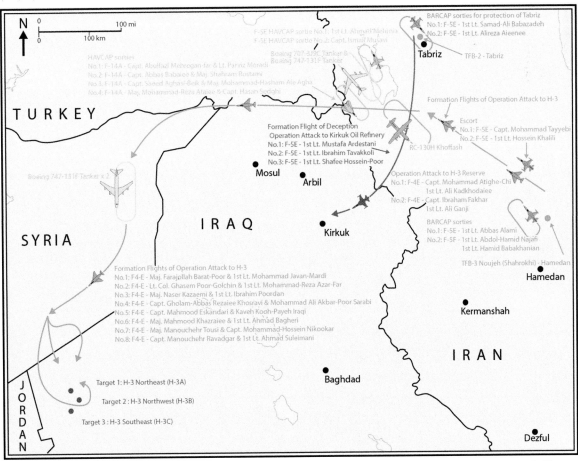

This detailed map shows the intricacies of one of the most complex air operations. Operation Attack on al-Walid AB. The flight paths of all participating F-4s, F-5s, F-14s, KC-707s, KC-747s and RC-130 are shown with the names of their pilots.
(Map be George Anderson)

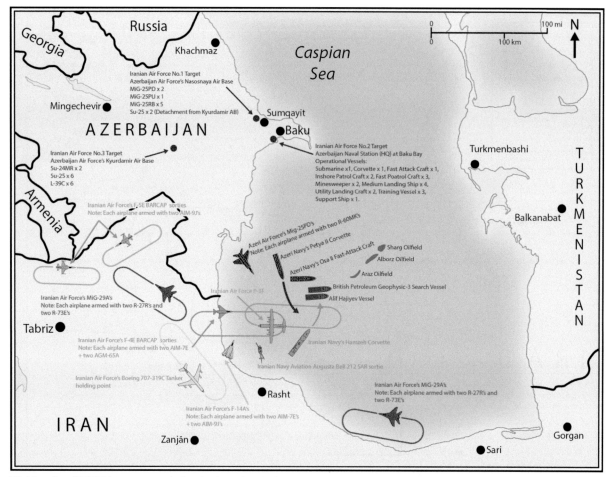

Flight paths of IRIAF interceptors during the Iran–Azerbaijan critical phase of the maritime dispute, 21 and 24 July 2001.
(Map by George Anderson)

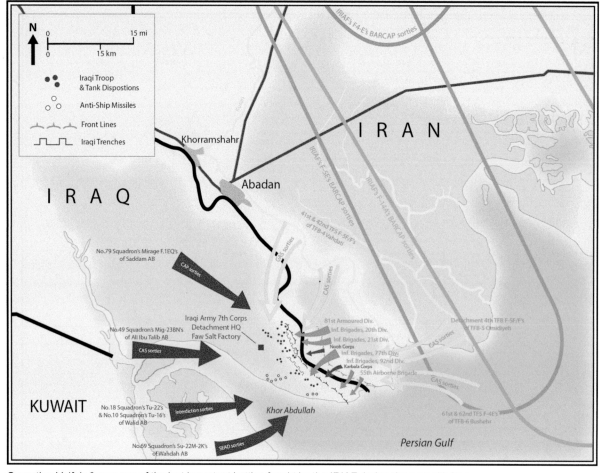

Operation Valfajr-8 was one of the last important battles fought by the IRIAF during the war with Iraq.
(Map by George Anderson)

Emblem of the TFB.3 Shahrokhi and its designer. (Babak Taghvaee Collection)

218 was a former IIAF F-5As of No. 2 based at Mafraq AB. This airplane was also sold to HAF in the latter half of the 1980. (via Ivo Sturzenegger via Claudio Maranta)

The Saeghe.II with 3-7181 serial number and one of the 23rd TFS's six F-5E Saeghes, both in Asian Minor II colors. In this photo they are holding in the quick check area of taxi way 15 at Mehrabad international airport prior take off and their participate in Iran's Military Day Parade 2015. (AMJT)

3-527 was one of last remaining F-5As in IIAF service, this photo was taken in Mehrabad airport in 1975, it and several other F-5A/Bs were ready for delivery to the RJAF. (Babak Taghvaee Collection).

3-7019 can be seen during take off from 29L RWY of Mehrabad international airport in April 2009. (Babak Taghvaee Collection)

This F-5B was originally operated by the IIAF, before being sent to South Vietnam during Operation Enhance Plus. It was returned to Iran in 1975 and was in the service of the Iran from 1979 to 1996 after which it was grounded. Rediscovered in 2008, together with a stock of 253 spare parts, it was brought to Mehrabad and completely rebuilt. It re-entered service as 3-7009B with the 43rd CCTS in 2010, but was grounded again three months later and has been used as source of spares ever since. (photo by Babak Taghvaee)

Prince Reza Pahlavi II is seen here with F-5F 3-7163 s/n (c/n: Z1010) during a cross-country flight from Tabriz to Kish Island in the Persian Gulf in the summer of 1977. He performed his first solo flight onboard another 21st TFS's F-5F with 3-7167 s/n (c/n: Z1014) on 14 March 1978. (Babak Taghvaee Collection)

Captain Sharifi-Ra'ad shot down a MiG-21MF on 26 November 1980. (Via Kouros Pashazadeh)

In November 1977 the IIAF performed a massive parade and its Golden Crown display team performed aerobatics for governmental authorities from Saudi Arabia, Qatar, UAE, Bahrain and Kuwait. Just weeks before the invitation by the Arab kings of the Middle East announced the inclusion of the Iranian triple Islands: Bumusa, Small Tunb and Large Tunb, as part of the UAE, therefore the Shah used the parade to showcase his country's air power. This photo was taken before the display at TFB.7 Shiraz. (www.iiaf.net)

1st Lieutenant Bijan Harooni death was in vain. His airplane was shot down by friendly fire and after his successful ejection he was killed by villagers mistaking him for an Iraqi; he was unconscious thus could not produce his ID card. (Babak Taghvaee Collection)

This photo shows one of the first restored former Ethiopian F-5Es, with Ataollah Mohebbi, a TFB.4-pilot. (Babak Taghvaee Collection)

The F-5E serialled 3-7052 was one of several Tiger IIs that IRIAF technicians restored to operational condition prior to Operation Shafagh, when it was used by the 42nd TFS. This photo shows it during the functional check flight (FCF) after its repairs. (Abdollah Bagheri-Ra'ad)

3-7302 was the second Azarakhsh manufactured by the Owj Complex. This photograph shows it with the first Owj Complex-built Saeghe (c/n S.110-001, serial 3-7366), during the exercise Zarbat-e-Zulfiqar, at TFD 2 in 2006. (Babak Taghvaee Collection)

During a ceremony the IRIAF unveiled second and third Saeghe prototypes on 20 September 2007. Iranian Army Chief Commander Lieutenant-General Ataollah Salehi and Minister of Defense Mostafa Mohammad Najjar visited all three prototypes of Saeghe-80 airplanes in Mehrabad airport. All three Saeghes were parked in TFB.1QRA Hardened Aircraft Shelters. (Photo by Babak Taghvaee)

During the unveiling ceremony of the second and third Saeghes, S.110-001 and Saeghe (S.110-002) performed several fly pasts over Mehrabad international airport on 20 September 2007. (Photo by Babak Taghvaee)

The first three manufactured Saeghes by Owj Complex are seen in the Caspian ramp of Mehrabad international airport in October 2007. (photo by Babak Taghvaee)

Nineteen F-5s of the 41st TFS are parked on TFB.4's main ramp during this photoshoot. The front airplane is SR.II serialled 3-7034, while another SR.II, fourteen F-5Es and four F-5Fs are in the line-up. (Photo by Abdol-Rahim Sharafi Farimani / IRIAF's Research and Studies office)

Tail art on the 41st TFS Tiger IIs. They were drawn on the vertical stabilizers of 12 F-5E/Fs after a request by Colonel Nader Yaghoubi before the IRIAF's gunnery competitions in 2009. (Photos by Babak Taghvaaee)

3-7025B with 11 Bort Number is the 11th and last IAMI-manufactured Simorgh. This airplane was constructed on 2-7212's airframe (a RF-5A). (Photo by Babak Taghvaee)

3-7162 (c/n: Z1009) is the closest F-5F to the camera. This airplane was lost during exercise Milade Noore Velayat and its pilot Colonel Qader Asadi was killed in June 2009. (Photo by Abdol-Rahim Sharafi Farimani / IRIAF's Research and Studies office)

3-7172 and 3-7154 can be seen during take off from TFB.4's runway. 3-7154's pilot was Colonel Hosssein Tahan-Nazif. (Photo by Babak Taghvaee)

Finally the IRIAF's deputy of operations ordered TFB.2 to color all its Saeghes in the three-tone Asian Minor II color scheme to take part in Iran's 2015 Military Day Parade. Here the 3-7369 can be seen after circling the Mehrabad international airport prior landing nine days before the parade on 9 April 2015. (Alireza Khodakarami)

The 3-7157 is the only F-5F of the 21st TFS stationed at the Mashhad air station. The 'aggressor' artwork on its vertical stabilizer was applied after its last overhaul in the air station's maintenance center in 2014. (AMJT via Facebook)

Captain Erfani's F-5E with serial number 3-7075 was damaged by an SA-7 during the mission against Buban military base at Halabche on 12 November 1980. He performed an emergency landing on the Maraghe highway; the next day an IRIAF CH-47C serialled 5-9302 brought his Tiger II back to TFB.2. (Babak Taghvaee Collection)

would be no MiG-23s around. We lacked the fuel to engage so I suggested to descend to low level. Few seconds later, Sharifi-Raad called, 'MiG, MiG, MiG!!!' We called him back but there was no response.

Iraqis shot him down and later in the day we flew a mission to find the wreck of his plane, but couldn't see anything.[*]

Combined with dozens of strikes against various enemy military bases and bridges, these attacks forced the Iraqis to withdraw large contingents of their air defence forces from the frontlines and deploy them to protect areas deep inside Iraq. This in turn made CAS sorties along the frontlines much less risky for the IRIAF pilots, enabling them to force the Iraqi army into withdrawal from Dezful and Susangerd.

LIBERATION OF SUSANGERD

Out of the three prongs of the Iraqi advance into the Khuzestan, only the one that resulted in the capture of the port of Khorramshahr proved successful. Iraqi attacks on Ahwaz and Dezful were thwarted by the IRIAF. During early November Baghdad turned its attention to Susangerd. On 16 November they broke the resistance of disorganized IRGC troops and captured much of the town.

Iraqi joy over this success was short-lived because they never managed to secure all of Susangerd due to the skilfull defence by several groups of local volunteers and a few minor army units, and because early the following morning they found themselves exposed to a fierce counter-attack by the 92nd Armoued Division and the IRIAF.

TFB.4 became involved in this battle on 16 November when its F-5Es

---

[*] Sharifi-Raad was badly injured during his low-altitude ejection and hit the ground very hard. He was recovered by sympathetic Kurdish insurgents and brought back to Iran a month later.

Two F-5 pilots were killed during operations related to the liberation of Susangerd: 1st Lieutenant Mohammad Kambakhsh Ziaee (left) on 16 November 1980 and Major Younes Khoshbin (right) on 18 November 1980. (Tom Cooper Archive)

flew a series of strikes against the 9th Iraqi Armoured Division, losing one Tiger II and its pilot – 1st Lieutenant Mohammad Kambakhsh – in the process. When the Iraqis attempted to reinforce this division with fresh troops the TFB.4 hit back in force, and F-5Es wiped out an entire column of the 12th Armoured Brigade that was approaching by road from Bostan. By 18 November the Iraqis were forced to fall back from Susangerd as the IrAF was thrown into the fray in an attempt to disrupt Iranian operations. Several of its formations beat a hasty retreat at the first sight of Iranian F-14 Tomcats, while one MiG-23 was shot down by the Hawk SAM site near Ahwaz. In return, the IRIAF lost the F-5E flown by Major Younes Khoshbin, who was killed. Overall, the recovery of Susangerd proved an early major success for the Iranian military and resulted in such enormous losses for the Iraqis that they never attempted to occupy this relatively isolated town again.

OPERATION NASSR

As soon as the Iranians managed to stop the Iraqi advances, public pressure forced the government in Tehran to launch a major counter-attack. Actually, the Iranian army was neither ready nor in any condition to force the Iraqis into a withdrawal to the border. Nevertheless, the plan for Operation Nassr, set for 17 December 1980, was set in motion and whatever forces were available went into action. According to this plan, the 1st and the 3rd Brigades of the 16th Armoured Division, and the 2nd Brigade of the 92nd Armoured Division, reinforced by the 231st Tank Battalion from the 77th Division, one battalion of the IRGC and a small guerrilla force led by Dr Mustafa Chamran, were to attack Iraqi positions in the Howeizeh area and liberate the Hamid military base before forcing the Iraqis to withdraw from Khuzestan completely.

The IRIAF was to provide CAS during this operation, foremost with F-5Es from TFB.4, although F-4 Phantoms from TFBs 3 and 6 would also participate. Because the IRIAF was not yet able of deploying its MIM-23B Hawk SAMs in sufficient numbers, F-14s from TFB.8 were tasked with providing top cover for ground forces, and were sometimes supported by F-5Es from TFB.4. On request from the intelligence and reconnaissacne command of the Iranian army, a direct air support centre (DASC) was set up in Ahwaz to control all aerial operations. This was supported by RC-130E/H Khoofash SIGINT-gathering aircraft of the IRIAF, which were responsible for tracking the activity of Iraqi SAM sites. Among other intelligence conducted by these aircraft it was revealed that the Iraqis had learned about the Iranian preparations and were in the process of reinforcing their ground forces in the targeted area. The Iranians also learned that the Iraqis had established a powerful air defence system over occupied parts of Khuzestan. Its centrepiece was two SA-6 SAM sites deployed at Allah-u-Akbar Heights, supported by one SA-3 SAM site further to the rear and several SA-2 sites positioned inside Iraq, along the border with Iran. Furthermore, the IrAF moved most of its MiG-21s of No. 9 Squadron to Abu Ubaydah AB near al-Kut.

Bad weather prevented the IRIAF from commencing its attacks on 20 December; attempts were made but most pilots failed to find their targets. As a result, the air force only went into action once the army had launched its offensive, on 25 December. On the first morning eight F-5Es bombed positions of the 1st Iraqi Mechanized Division with BLU-1Bs and BL.755s. During the following days IRIAF activity remained limited to a few CAS missions. On 30 December two Tigers were scrambled to support a lone F-4E from the 31st TFS, which was attempting to intercept two Iraqi Tupolev Tu-22 bombers and four MiG-23BNs that were approaching the combat zone.

Serious action began on 1 January 1981 when TFB.4 was tasked to hit the Iraqi 5th Mechanized Infantry Division in the al-Halfaya area that was rushing to reinforce the 9th Armoured Division. This mission was flown by four F-5Es and hit the enemy hard, destroying several dozen vehicles. During the following days, additional strikes – sometimes including up to 10 F-5Es, and often in combination with F-4Es from other bases – were flown against local Iraqi HQs. One Tiger II was shot down on 5 January when the plane, flown by 1st Lieutenant Mahmood Yazdi, was hit by SA-6s near Allah-u-Akbar Heights. The pilot ejected but was injured on landing; he was recovered by Iranian ground forces.

Two days later, TFB.4 launched eight F-5Es to attack the 3rd Battalion of the Iraqi 9th Armoured Division, positioned west of Hamid military base. Using Mk.82s with snake-eye retarding fins (Mk.82SEs), CBUs and napalm bombs, the Tigers mauled the Iraqi unit, causing it up to 40 percent losses. However, once again, the SA-6s shot down an F-5E, that of Captain Mahmoud Yazdan-Panah who was killed when his Tiger II serial number 3-7016 received a direct hit.

On 8 January, all F-4Es from the 32nd TFS and four F-4Ds from the 11th Combat Command Training Squadron (CCTS) were forward deployed to TFB.4 in order to better support the Tigers. Vahdati thus managed to launch a total of 13 Phantoms and 14 Tigers into CAS missions for Iranian ground forces south of Ahwaz and near Abaviyah that day. However, one F-4Es serial 3-6613 was shot down by SA-6s, while another was damaged by flak, and an F-5E was forced to make an emergency landing after suffering damage to both engines. Furthermore, one F-4D (serial 3-6714) was shot down the following day.

The situation on the ground was not progressing well for the Iranians due to their attack literally being bogged down in the mud, and to the deployment of Iraqi T-72 MBTs and the massive volume of Iraqi artillery fire. The army thus called for the IRIAF to provide cover for its retreating units and the F-5s – with F-4s – spent most of 9 January bombing Iraqi army forces around Umm-Alaqar, Abaviyah, and south of Susangerd. Once again, losses were heavy. The IRIAF lost three Phantoms. On a more positive note for the Iranians, the Iraqi counter-attack into the southern flank of the Iranian army formations was stopped dead, and one F-14A providing top cover destroyed two Iraqi MiG-23s using AIM-54A Phoenix missiles.

Above left: On 5 January 1981 1st Lieutenant Mahmood Yazdi's F-5E was shot down and killed by an SA-6 SAM near the Allah-Akbar Heights. (Babak Taghvaee Collection)

Above right: 1st Lieutenant Mohammad-Hossein Darabi Soufiany's F-5E was shot down by an SA-6 during Operation Raqqabiyah – a minor offensive aimed at streamlining the frontline of the 16th Armoured Division in western Khuzestan – on 18 March 1981. (via Tom Cooper Archive)

In all, Operation Nassr, or Howeyzeh – as it is known in the West – failed. Following initial success, Iranian forces had to withdraw from the battlefield after suffering significant losses. The IRIAF flew about 200 CAS and interdiction sorties, and 471 CAPs, but lost two F-5Es (with one of their pilots) and five F-4s for little gain.

In March 1981 the Iranian army established its first major formation since the revolution, the 21st Hamzeh Infantry Division, consisting largely of elements of the former Shah's Guard. The first major operation of this division was Operation Tappeh Cheshmeh. The operation focused on clearing a number of Iraqi strongholds in Septoon Heights, reaching the Naderi Bridge and establishing contact with the 84th Infantry Division that fought in the Khorramabad area, further north. The attack was launched on 4 April 1981 andwas initially strongly supported by F-5Es from TFB.4. However, the Iraqis moved several SA-2, SA-3 and SA-6 SAM sites into the area, prompting the IRIAF to deploy unmanned aerial vehicles (UAVs) in combination with RF-5As to search for missile sites. During the following days, 10 out of 19 UAVs were shot down by Iraqis, nine were recovered by the Iranians, but none of the RF-5As were hit and all Iraqi SAM sites were located and repeatedly shelled by Iranian artillery. The Iraqis countered by attacking TFB.4 with several SS-1c Scud-B SSMs, but failed to cause any serious damage.

THE H-3 BLITZ

In early April 1981, F-5Es participated in a major attack against the Iraqi air base complex known as H-3 in the west and locally designated al-Wallid air base. Situated near the old British-built pipeline connecting central Iraq with the port of Haifa in Palestine, and some 20 kilometres east of the border with Jordan, H-3 was originally a pumping station with a small dirt strip. After becoming the scene of several fierce air battles between the IrAF and the Israeli Air Force during the June 1967 War, H-3 was expanded into a major air base, and by 1980 received two dispersal sites nearby. Early during the war with Iran, the H-3 complex was used by Iraqis as a depot to distribute its transport and bomber units, which came under severe pressure because of repeated IRIAF air strikes on air bases in central Iraq. Subsequently, it became a rear base for unserviceable IrAF combat aircraft, but also deployed MiG-23 interceptors for defence from frequent forays by Israeli reconnaissance fighters. This was not the only reason for the Iranians deciding to hit this complex. The H-3 complex was on the other side of Iraq, far away from Iran's borders, and thus appeared untouchable to the IRIAF. This was an important factor because the failure of Operation Nassr had lowered the morale of the Iranian armed forces. Not only that, the Iraqis managed to defend their positions on occupied Iranian ground and it appeared as as though Iran was on the brink of losing the war. Therefore, the IRIAF high command was ready to put significant forces at risk for this operation – officially named Operation Attack on al-Wallid, but unofficially known as the H-3 Blitz – very much with the intention of making it a major morale booster.

TFB.4 student pilots in 1981/1982 pose in front of F-5F serialled 3-7154 (first manufactured F-5F in the world). Standing: Bijan Tavakkoli, Dallal Khoush, Fatemi, Asad-Zadeh, Mighani (he would go on to become commander of the IRIAF) and Shahsavari. Sitting: Bikarani, Ranjbaran, Vahidi-Ra'ad, Shabani and Hadiyan. (via Naser Majdani)

Because of the sensitivity of the operation and its complex procedures, commands for the engaging forces were issued only as the pilots and crews were on their way to their target. The codes issued to F-5 participants were Nader for the pair of Tiger IIs flying a CAP near Tabriz, and Hormuz for F-5Es flying a diversionary attack on Kirkuk oil refinery.

The operation was launched on 4 April 1981 at 0430 when eleven F-5s launched from TFB.2: Colonel Abraham Ghorbani flew weather reconnaissance in an F-5F, four F-5Es flew escort for F-4s and Boeing tankers, two F-5Es flew a CAP over Tabriz, while three F-5Es – led by 1st Lieutenant Mustafa Ardestani – launched an attack on the Kirkuk oil refinery. Captain Mohammad Tayyebi flew escort for F-4s, and recalled:

> Major Yadollah Rastegar-Far, Deputy Director Operations at TFB.2, called me at 20.00hrs in the evening of 29 March, and ordered me to report at the CP. There I joined five other F-5E-pilots, and was ordered to go to TFB.3 on the next morning. From Nojeh, we did several familiarization flights and met pilots from the 31st and the 32nd TFS, but nobody knew the reason for all of this....
> We returned to TFB.2 and were put into the QRA shift, everything was normal – until the evening of 3 April, when Col Baratpour arrived to tell me that the TFB.3 could have a mission for us on the next day, which would consist of F-5Es escorting Phantoms in Ourumiyeh area... We flew that mission as ordered, in complete radio silence...*

---

* Mohammad Tayyebi survived the war with Iraq and retired with the rank of brigadier-general.

The attack on Kirkuk was highly successful, especially with regard to distracting the attentions of the Iraqi air defences from the formation of eight F-4Es that was refuelling from a Boeing 707-3J9C tanker at low altitude over Ourumiyeh Lake. Protected by a pair of F-14As, the Phantoms then flew low along the Iraqi-Turkish border until reaching Syrian airspace. After taking fuel from two Boeing 747-131F tankers, they then attacked al-Wallid ABs. This attack caught the Iraqis completely off guard. Iranian pilots later reported sighting of at least 48 different transports, bombers, fighter bombers and helicopters, and were credited with the destruction of 10 MiG-21 interceptors, one Tu-22 bomber, 15 Mi-17 and Mi-2 helicopters on the ground, together with one armament storage depot and an approach control radar. While the Iraqis denied suffering a single loss, they received such a psychological blow that during the following years Baghdad invested billions in the construction of a semi-automatic integrated air-defence system at Kari, and purchased 18,000 surface-to-air missiles.

REDUCING ACTIVITY

During the first months of the war, the IRIAF, the IRIAA and a few scattered units of the Iranian army managed to stop the Iraqi invasion of Khuzestan and Kermanshah. Flying thousands of CAPs, CAS sorties, interdiction strikes, reconnaissance and even anti-ship missions, the air force managed to paralyze large parts of the Iraqi economy, establish air superiority over the battlefield, cut off the fuel supply to advancing Iraqi ground forces, and then impose heavy attrition upon the latter. However, this success came at a high price as dozens of aircraft and pilots were lost.

The F-5 units of the IRIAF suffered higher losses than any other squadrons; between 25 June 1980 and 18 March 1981 52 F-5Es and two F-5Fs were written off. Forty of them were from TFB.4. If they'd had the full logistics support from the USA that the air force originally intended such losses would have been easy to replace.

Although its total manpower was reduced to 35,000 by September 1980, the IRIAF was still in possession of enough pilots and ground personnel, even after all the post-revolutionary purges, to maintain the advantage. However, because the Iranian government had cut all relations with the USA, no replacement aircraft could be obtained. The IRIAF thus found itself facing an enemy without this insurmountable obstruction: on the contrary, France and the Soviet Union were rapidly replenishing all the IrAF aircraft as they were destroyed.

This realization forced the IRIAF to introduce several measures, including a complete revision of its tactics and implementation of lessons learned during the early months of the war, and a massive reduction in activity in order to preserve its surviving assets. Because there was a severe lack of experienced and skilled commanders, a commission was established that reviewed all dismissals from 1979 and 1980. The young Commander-in-Chief of the IRIAF, Colonel Fakkouri, personally attempted to appease many of the dismissed personnel in an effort to bring them back into IRIAF service. This decision came very late though, and not all dismissed officers and other ranks decided to rejoin; indeed, by 1981 thousands of them had left Iran.

Except for the lack of executive officers, the IRIAF was facing a mass of other problems. Most important among them was that all training and further development of the air force had been cancelled in 1979. Although all available personnel had undergone some refresher training since the start of hostilities, this was by no means enough, and during the first few months of the war there was no time to do it. By March 1981 most air force personnel were exhausted, in need of rest and recuperation as well as refresher training. In April the IRIAF high command therefore made the decision to cut the number of combat sorties by half, thus decreasing the workload of the entire force, while simultaneously restarting training exercises and heeding the need for the acquisition of replacement equipment. A result related to this decision was to reactivate all 11 F-5Bs transferred to Mehrabad in the summer of 1980 and assign them to the 11th CCTS, where they were used for training new pilots – exclusively cadets whose training in the USA had been interrupted by the revolution. At least 10 newly trained pilots had joined TFB.4 by the end of 1981, by which time a new programme for advanced flight and gunnery training was in place. Combined with more intensive refresher training of qualified pilots and ground personnel, this reduced the number of accidents to zero by early 1982.

OPERATION SHABAH-2

During March 1981, the Iranian army prepared an offensive – Operation Shabah-2 (Phantom II) – against a concentration of Iraqi military east of the Karoun River, north of Kharkhe-Koor and southwest of Ahwaz. The IRIAF was tasked with providing CAS and reconnaissance. For this purpose the air force high command decided to reinforce the battered F-5-units at Vahdati through more intensive barrier-combat air patrols (BARCAP) flown by F-14As.

Operation Shabah-2 was launched on 21 August 1981. Tigers initially bombed the Iraqi position around Shadgan, Darkhovin, and Suleimaniyah, while RF-5As ran a number of recce sorties. However, contrary to earlier on in the war, the tempo of the operation was

Major Mehdi Bakhshandeh, a pilot from 11th TRS, was killed during a recce sortie over the Marivan area on 17 July 1981. His RF-5A (serial 2-7201) was shot down by friendly fire over the Qom Salt Lake. (via Tom Cooper Archive)

significantly decreased; by mid-September 1981 TFB.4 had only launched 86 CAS sorties, expending 373,526lbs of ammunition in the process. Despite this the IRIAF caused much trouble for the Iraqis. The supporting F-14s had scored a number of MiG kills over the battlefield, and the F-5s had hit the Iraqis so heavily that the CO of the Iraqi 10th Armoured Division ordered his long-range artillery to open fire at Vahdati AB on 25 September 1981. While some of shells fell near the armament depot, destroying six boxes with Mk.81 bombs and killing airman Gholam-Reza Allah-Morad, no other serious damage was caused.

Learning of the Iranian army's troubles, the IrAF launched dozens of fighter bombers to strike back, provoking a number of air contacts over the following days. Tiger II pilots from TFB.4 were usually deployed to fly low-altitude CAPs, but their planes proved too slow to catch the much faster MiGs and Sukhois. However, armed with the AIM-54 Phoenix long-range AAMS, the Tomcats scored seven confirmed kills against Iraqi fighter bombers between 28 August and 30 September.

Overall, despite this minimalistic approach, the IRIAF's participation in Operation Shabah-2 proved very successful. Not only had the Iraqis suffered additional losses to air strikes by F-5Es – including 160 MBTs and 30 other vehicles – but the air force had not lost any of its fighter jets, while the army had liberated 150 square kilometres of Khuzestan.

Emboldened, the Iranian government then ordered the army to continue this operation and the latter thus launched the Offensive Shabah-2/Part 2 (or Samen-al-Aemmeh or Tariq al-Quds) on 29 November 1981. During the course of this offensive the reformed 16th and 92nd Armoured Divisions forced the Iraqis to abandon all their positions between Howeizeh and Susangerd in the north, and Allah-u-Akbar Heights and al-Halfaya in the south.

The IRIAF continued operating in its earlier restrictive fashion, but even so deployed 57 aircraft in support of Shabah-2. New to this operation was the appearance of two battalions of MIM-23B I-Hawk SAMs, deployed near Dez Dam and Fuly Abad to support the F-14s and F-5s flying CAPs. Such reinforcement was sorely needed as the IrAF was about to introduce several powerful new weapons' systems.

The first of these were Dassault Mirage F.1EQs, armed with French-made Matra Super 530F-1 medium-range AAMs and flown by pilots that had received excellent air-combat training in France. In an attempt to open safe routes for the MiG and Sukhoi fighter bombers, pilots of the No. 79 Squadron – the first Iraqi unit to operate this type – primarily concentrated on taking out BARCAP, flying F-14s. The second major new weapons' system in Iraqi hands

لف ، الف. (لیست آماج) به ضمیمه ۲ (آتش پشتیبانی هوائی) به پیوست ت (طرح پشتیبانی آتش) به طـرح عملیاتـی کربلا ۳

ملاحظات	سمت حمله به توپ به شکل هدن	زمان اجرای آتش TOT	اندازه هدف	مختصات هدف E طول	N عرض	شمــــاره هدف	رمــز هدف	دین
ارتع پائین	شمالی جنوبی		—	٤٨١٠١٠	٣١٠٤٣٠	۱۹ تانگ و ۱٦ نفـربر	علم	۱
//	آزاد	بشعاع ٥٠/۱کیلو	٤٨١٤٢٠	٣١٠٩٢٥	٣٥ تانگ و ۱۲ نفر و ۲۲ خودرو	صنعت	۲
//	آزاد	بشعاع ٥٠٠متر	٤٨٠٧٠٥	٣١١٠١٥	۳۰ تانگ و ۵ نفربر	تجربه	۳
//	شمالی جنوبی	٥٠٠×۱٠٠متر	٤٨٠٧٥٠	٣١١٢٤٠	۲۳ تانگ و ۱۰ خودرو	اعتقاد	٤
//	شرقی غربی	بشعاع۱کیلومتر	٤٨٠٧٥٠	٣١١١١٥	۱٤ تانگ و ۱۳ نفـربر	ایمان	٥
//	شرقی غربی	بشعاع ۲ کیلومتر	٤٨٠٥٠٠	٣١١١٠٥	نقطه آباد درپوفیر	سواد	٦
//	آزاد	بشعاع ٥٠٠متر	٤٨٠٤٣٠	٣١١٠٣٥	۱۰ تانگ و موضع سام ۲ وبریا ٦سکوی پرتاب	روحیه	۷
//	آزاد	بشعاع ٣٠٠متر	٤٨٠٥٥٥	٣١١٠٠٥	موضع سام ۲ پربسا ٦ سکوی پرتاب	شهامت	۸

This is a scan of the Karbala-3 combat command frag order attachment giving details of the IRIAF's CAS sorties during operation Beit al-Moghaddas. (Babak Taghvaee Collection)

was the Soviet-made Kh-28E anti-radar missile deployed by Su-22M-2Ks of No. 5 Squadron IrAF. These Sukhois and their Kh-28Es were used to knock out high-power acquisition radars (HIPARs) of Iranian MIM-23 sites in advance of any incoming Iraqi air strike.

Combat operations related to Shabah-2 commenced on 27 October, when Iraqis used their Kh-28Es for the first time to destroy at least six Iranian HIPARs. While IRIAF F-14s had managed to shoot down an attacking Sukhois, the Hawk crews subsequently changed tactics; they would switch the working mode of their radars to standby at the first appearance of Iraqi fighter bombers. The defence of the sites would then be taken over by two F-5Es flying a CAP nearby.

Two weeks later the Tiger IIs received a new task. On 15 November 1981 the IrAF Mirages managed to shoot down two F-14As by approaching at low altitude before climbing and attacking from below – well outside the envelope of the Tomcat's radars and weapons. This prompted the IRIAF to task F-5Es with flying additional low-altitude CAPs in order to cover possible Iraqi ingress routes toward F-14s.

Finally, the F-5Es were tasked with the mission of protecting RF-4Es that were making reconnaissance runs over the battlefield and support F-4Es from TFB.3 forward deployed at Vahdati.

This new organization of the Iranian air defences proved highly successful. On 25 November the forward-deployed Phantoms enjoyed a highly successful day when they shot down four MiGs and Sukhois, followed by the downing of two MiG-23MSs by Tomcats that then went on to kill a brand-new Iraqi MiG-23ML on intelligence provided by low-flying F-5Es. In turn, one of the F-5E pilots from Vahdati, successfully vectored by Tomcat crews and the ground control from Dezful, intercepted an Iraqi MiG, which was shot down with the help of an

بكلی سری

ضمـ ۱ (آتش پشتیبانی هوائی) به پیوست ت (طرح پشتیبانی آتش) بطرح عملیاتی کربلا ۳

This scan of the Karbala-3 frag order contains a table of primary targets for the first week of the operation. It shows details of the targets, the radius of the target distribution, their exact coordinates, call-signs, the position of attack to the targets and target-bombing tactics. (Babak Taghvaee Collection)

AIM-9J sidewinder on 29 November.

By 2 December the IrAF pilots had become so nervous about this effective triangulation that all four Su-22s beat a hasty retreat at the first sign of Tomcats. When, several hours later, Iraqi MiG-23MS interceptors returned to attack F-14s they were detected early and one was shot down; on the following day Tomcats dealt with two Mirages in a similar fashion.*

On 5 December 1981 two Su-22s attacking the Hawk site near Fuly Abad were shot down, one by an F-14A. The Iraqis briefly evened the score that afternoon when Mirages sneaked into Iranian airspace and shot down two F-14s with the help of Super 530F-1s. Later the MIM-23 sites downed four IrAF fighter bombers.

Operation Shabah-2/Part-2 ended on 14 December with results that were satisfactory to the Iranians. In exchange for the loss of four F-14s and six HIPAR radars, the IRIAF had established air superiority, enabling the army to relieve the sieges of Abadan, Bostan and Susangerd, and scatter major Iraqi army concentrations in Khuzestan, pushing them toward the Hawizeh Marshes.

OPERATION SHABAH-3
(BEIT AL-MOGHADDAS AND FAT'H AL-MOBIN)

Emboldened by the success of Shabah-2, the Iranians began preparations to liberate Khorramshar and push the Iraqis out of southwestern Khuzestan in early 1982. For the purpose of controlling forces in the coming offensive, the army and the IRGC established the Karbala Joint HQ and four forward CPs, which included officers from all involved branches of the military. The commander of the IRIAF assets, Colonel Bahram Hooshyar, set up his HQ at Vahdati, from where he controlled the organization and tasks of four 'fire-support units' (F-4 and F-5 fighter bombers), three air-defence units (F-4s and F-14s), the Dezful Air Defence Group (early warning radar unit, one Hawk SAM site, one Sky Guard/Oerlikon flak battery and one ZU-23 flak battery), and the Ahwaz Air Defence Group (one early warning radar unit, one Sky Guard/Oerlikon flak battery and one ZU-23 flak battery), plus assorted reconnaissance, support and liaison assets.

Launched on 30 April 1982 following a period of frenetic activity by the IRIAF, Shabah-3 began with powerful attacks from RF-4Es, supported by 20 daily CAS sorties – flown by F-4s and F-5s from TFB. Because of the proximity of the battlefield to Vahdati AB, many of the Tiger IIs were armed with up to nine Mk.82 bombs (similarly, F-4Es were carrying as many as 24).

As before, the IRIAF deployed its combination of SAMs, low-flying F-5s and high-flying F-14s, and the system proved so effective that the IrAF fighter bombers rarely approached the battlefield. With their backs against the Hawizeh Marshes, three Iraqi army divisions collapsed. Nearly 15,000 officers and other ranks of the 3rd Armoured and the 5th Mechanized divisions surrendered, together with most of their heavy equiment. The rest of the Iraqi army retreated, withdrawing to positions behind the international border.

Iranian fighter bombers flew 130 CAS and interdiction sorties during this operation, deploying a total of 387,672lbs of bombs and rockets. Although the IRIAF proved unable to establish an IADS over the combat zone and was forced to continue deploying precious

F-14s to fill the gap caused by the lack of SAM sites, once again the combination of available assets proved effective. It not only shot down 55 IrAF fighter bombers (six Iraqi pilots were captured), but effectively paralyzed enemy air force combat operations. In return, it lost four F-4Es (two shot down by Mirages) and one HIPAR radar which was rapidly replaced. Units equipped with Tiger IIs did not suffer any losses during Shabah-3, but the F-5E flown by Rahim Zoghi was shot down over Iraq on 21 July 1982 while supporting the first Iranian ground attacks into Iraq.

LACK OF SPARES

By the time Shabah-3 was concluded, the IRIAF F-5 units were in poor condition. Of course many planes had been destroyed but dozens were damaged and in need of urgent repair. The US-imposed arms embargo, a result of the 1979 US embassy hostage crisis, had created a lack of spare parts for avionic systems – mainly Emerson AN/APQ-153 and AN/APQ-157 radars, Litton LN-33 INS and AN/ARN-84(V) TACAN platforms – which resulted in the number of mission-capable F-5E/Fs decreasing to unprecedented levels. For example, at the start of Shabah-3, out of 40 F-5Es and 20 F-5Fs at TFB.4, only eight were in mission-capable condition. The condition of 35 F-5Es and the six F-5Fs still available at TFB.2 was only slightly better; while 41 were flyable, only 20 were mission-capable. The number of combat-ready F-5 pilots declined too; only 51 were left at TFB.4 and even fewer at TFB.2.

It was already in early 1982 that the IRIAF was thus forced to disband the 23rd TFS and the 43rd TTS, and re-distribute their aircraft to other squadrons. By the end of the Operation Shabah-3, the situation had reached such a state of urgency that the air force's primary focus became hunting down spares. However, none were to be found within the ALS. Brazil, Malaysia and Saudi Arabia, the only other countries operating similarly equipped F-5E/Fs, turned down all Iranian requests for assistance.

Some *homafars* who had helped the new government purge the air force, came up with an idea to solve the problem of the dire lack of spares – the Self-Sufficiency Jihad Division (SSJD). However, while officially responsible for the local manufacturing of spare parts and for the development of new systems, assemblies and even upgrades for available aircraft, most early activities of the SSJD were fruitless, at least inconsistent, and usually little more than propaganda. For much of the first half of the 1980s the IRIAF was forced to solve most of its spares' problems through clandestine acquisition abroad – usually via various British, Israeli and US brokers. The air force spent much of 1982 using spares obtained in this manner to repair, and return to service, as many Tiger IIs as possible. With the ranks of their depleted units refilled the pilots from TFB.2 and TFB.4 even ran a number of intense exercises during that year – between combat operations. For example, F-5 pilots from Tabriz organized themselves into cells of four, each practising gunnery, navigation, bombing and other skills while other cells flew combat sorties.

During the same year, Tehran also reached an agreement with Switzerland for the delivery of 80 Pilatus PC-7 training aircraft. Two F-5 pilots from the 21st and the 22nd TFS were sent to Switzerland on an instructor pilot course, and helped deliver the first batch of five PC-7Cs to Iran in 1983. A further 35 Swiss trainers followed in 1984, but then their deliveries stopped due to immense pressure from the USA who claimed the Iranians intended to use these aircraft for suicide attacks on US Navy warships.

---

* Miraculously, a Mirage pilot – Abd al-Ghani Seyed al-Dulaiymi – survived a Phoenix strike on his aircraft, ejected safely and was captured by troops of the 92nd Armoured Division.

A group of 42nd TFS pilots in front of 3-7086 (c/n: U1074). (Babak Taghvaee Collection)

Before the Islamic revolution, Plant No.2 of IACI Co (Iranian Aircraft Industries) had the ability to overhaul all J-85 turbojet engine models. On the left is Master Sergeant Ali Ghlam-Ali who was the IIAF's representative at the IACI. He was the IIAF's sheet metal specialist. He had acquired experience in the Lockheed C-130 assembly line and later built all the pylons and adaptors of Iranian-made air-to-ground and air-to-air missiles during the war with Iraq.
(Ali Gholam-Ali archive)

To clarify blurred and messy relationships: after the revolution, the new regime cancelled several arms contracts including ones for the acquisition of parts, but later, after religious and Marxist students led by Khomeini and Masoud Rajavi (leader of MKO or Mujahedin Khalq Organization, the second-most important party of the Islamic revolution) attacked the US embassy and took 66 Americans hostage in November 1979, the US government subsequently imposed arms sanctions on the IRI regime.

In 1983, when the majority of F-5 parts available in IRIAF stocks had been used up, the IRIAF's representatives in the IRIAF's logistic support centre office in the NIOC's building in London attempted to acquire F-5 parts directly from the US for first time. But later their movement was tracked and by January 1984 all purchased parts were embargoed in the US before transfer to London. When this initial attempt failed, IRIAF's deputy of support and logistics decided to acquire parts through countries such as South Korea and Taiwan. South Korea shipped a series of F-5 spare-part batches to Iran in 1983 and 1984, using Indonesia as the fake destination. According to statements from South Korean authorities, high-ranking South Korean officials were bribed to fill out the export documents, but in reality the South Korean government was directly involved.

However, in early 1984, the US and Saudi Arabia (the Wahhabi regime was a supporter of Saddam Hussein) began pressurizing Seoul to terminate its arm sales. But the Koreans continued providing F-4 and F-5 parts to the IRIAF. The simple fact was that Air Korea was producing KF-5E/Fs under Northrop licence and had a large surplus. Later Taiwan and Singapore also began supplying F-5 parts to the IRIAF. Taiwan's AIDC (Aero Industries Department Centre) was producing F-5E/Fs for ROCAF (Republic of China Air Force) while Singapore Aircraft Industries was assembling or producing under licence avionics parts for Iranian F-5s. However, none of this was significant and anyway, by 1986, the US had halted any supplies from these three Asian countries.

The third method of procurement was through middlemen or arms dealers. For example, one of these brokers was Amir Masoud Motamedi who regularly shipped F-4, F-5, F-14, C-130 and P-3 parts before his arrest in 1985. Dozens of British, French, Israeli and Iranian brokers were involved in the IRIAF's F-5 parts procurement during the war.

EXPENSIVE ETHIOPIAN JUNK

One of the most famous cases of Iranians bypassing the US arms embargo occurred between 1984 and 1989 when Iran – with the help of arms brokers from Israel and Lebanon – managed to secure the delivery of five F-5Es, 11 F-5As, one F-5B and one RF-5A from Ethiopia.

During the 1960s and early 1970s Ethiopia was a major US and Iranian ally, and as such received extensive amounts of surplus military equipment from both countries. In 1974, Emperor Haile Selassie of Ethiopia was overthrown and during the subsequent power struggle a new government emerged that – because of the Somali invasion of Ogaden in July 1977 – declared itself Marxist-Leninist in order to secure political and military support from the USSR. During the following years this government purchased immense quantities of armament from the Soviets and ended up heavily indebted, but in possession of 14 surplus F-5As, one RF-5A, three F-5Bs and five F-5Es, for which it lacked spares because of the US arms embargo. In 1984 the government in Addis Ababa put these aircraft – stored in the open and in cases in terrible condition – up for sale.

While the government of Thailand was the first to show interest, the experts of the Royal Thai Air Force found the Ethiopian Freedom Fighters and Tiger IIs in such a terrible state that they refused to buy them. In order to remove them from the market, the CIA offered to buy them from the Ethiopians for US$7 million. However, around the same time the officials in Addis Ababa were contacted by an Israeli middleman, who offered them $68 million for four F-5Es alone. Surprised, but in need of cash, the Ethiopians accepted and – after receiving an advance payment of half the sum from an NIOC account – they delivered the aircraft in question, per ship, from Assab to Bandar Abbas.

The IRIAF technicians found the four ex-Ethiopian Tiger IIs to be in nearly unserviceable condition. While having only 497 hours' flying time on average on the airframe, they had suffered continuous exposrure to the elements. They all lacked their M39 cannons and most of of the avionics and logbooks. Initially, the Iranians refused to accept the aircraft, but eventually a solution was found; the 11 F-5As and single RF-5A would be thrown into a new deal for $34 million which the NIOC had already transferred to Ethiopia. The Freedom Fighers were shipped to Iran in two batches in 1985 and 1987, while the last Ethiopian F-5E reached Iran in late 1989.

All five F-5Es were brought to Vahdati, overhauled, completely restored by technicians and returned to service as 3-7182 to 3-7186. Eight F-5As were restored between 1985 and 1989 to serve as advanced trainers, and received serials 2-7250 to 2-7257. However, the extension of the work necessary to return them to service was such that none of them could be deployed in combat against Iraq.

NEW AGE

The period of reduced combat activity, overhauls and training had given some IRIAF pilots time to rethink their positions within the new government. Iraj Fazeli, one of most distinguished pilots from TFB.2, concluded that his life was under threat and defected with an F-5E to Turkey on 10 July 1983. In early 1984, two other pilots fled to Saudi Arabia, flying an F-5F. While all pilots were granted political asylum by local authorities, both aircraft were later returned to Iran.

Tiger II units were thus back to limited action toward the end of 1983, flying sorties in preparation for the first major Iranian offensive into Iraq, Operation Khaiber. They were now less often deployed for ground attacks and primarily served as point-defence interceptors. During an Iraqi attack on Ahwaz IAP the F-5E flown by Captain Ibrahim Bazargan was shot down by an Iraqi MiG-21 on 13 November 1983.

Launched on 22 February 1984, Khaiber was different in that the regular Iranian military would provide the primary support for six IRGC divisions deployed to launch an amphibious assault into Iraq through the Hawizeh Marshes. In several cases, IRIAA helicopters – protected by IRIAF interceptors – were used for the heliborne deployment of large numbers of ground units. The F-5Es from TFB.4 flew only a limited number of CAS sorties, while those from TFB.2 did not get involved in related operations but suffered a spate of accidents and near-fatal combat losses. The F-5E flown by Captain Ali-Asghar Hagh Madad-Milani was damaged during a mission deep into Iraq on 24 February and was forced to make an emergency landing on the Mahabad–Miandoab road. The plane was extensively damaged and the pilot badly injured. A few days later, Mansour Barikani crashed near TFB.2, writing off another F-5E, and there is another report concerning a collision between aircraft flown by Major Rostam Ibrahimzadeh Gonbadi and Captain Mansour Sobutipour near Tabriz during the course of a CAP sortie.

Combat air patrols inside Iranian airspace remained the main task of Iranian Tiger IIs during 1985 too, though they were deployed for some strikes into Iraq. For example, Ali-Asghar Saleh Ardestani and Javad Mohammadian bombed the Ali-Gharbi power plant on 4 March. Ardestani's plane was hit by at least one SA-7, causing the loss of both engines; the pilot managed to eject safely over Iranian territory and was recovered.

It was around this time that in response to IRGC firing SS-1c Scud-B SSMs obtained from Libya on Baghdad, Iraq initiated the campaign of attacks on cities and towns in Iran, known as the War of Cities. Initially, the IrAF primarily deployed MiG-25RB reconnaissance fighters of its No. 84 Squadron – equipped with the Peleng-D nav/attack platform and FAB-500T bombs – for attacks on Tehran, Esfahan and Shiraz. The CO of No. 84 Squadron flew the first mission against Tehran on 13 March 1985. He approached the Iranian capital at a speed of Mach 2.3 and an altitude of 21,000 metres before releasing his bombs 47 kilometres away from the target – the IRIAF HQ at Dowshan Tappeh. However, because Peleng-D was originally designed for the deployment of nuclear weapons, it was notoriously inprecise and FAB-500Ts released in this fashion regularly hit the ground anywhere within 10 kilometres of the actual target.[*]

Interceptions of MiG-25s proved extremely complex and troublesome for the IRIAF. Well informed about the detection capabilities of the Iranian ground-based, early-warning radar network, the Iraqis planned their missions to leave the IRIAF with the narrowest possible reaction time. By exploiting such gaps, and then flying high very fast, they left Iranian interceptors precious little time to reach a position from which they could effectively deploy their air-to-air missiles. Iran scored at least two confirmed kills against MiG-25s in 1982. F-14 Tomcats and their AIM-54 Phoenix missiles also proved capable after accelerating rapidly and climbing to a position almost directly in front of the oncoming enemy aircraft. However, if facing strong opposition, the Iraqi MiG-

---

[*] Brigadier-General Ahmad Sadik (IrAF, ret.), interview with Tom Cooper, March 2005.

25 pilots were advised to abort their mission.

Because attacks on Iranian cities were causing regular civilian casualties, IRIAF F-4 and F-5 crews demanded involvment resulting in Foxbat-Hunt. They were scrambled hundreds of times – usually without success; most times they would run out of fuel while still climbing toward their targets. Furthermore, when the Iraqis noticed scrambles of even F-5s in reaction to operations by MiG-25RBs, they would set up a trap for Iranian pilots. On 3 June 1985 the IrAF deployed a MiG-25PD interceptor instead of a bomber, catching the F-5E flown by Hassan Hossein-Zadeh while the Iranian was climbing to intercept, and shot it down with two R-40 AAMs.

Furthermore, aiming to realize Baghdad's empty claims of an airspace blockade to all international traffic over Iran, Iraqi MiG-25 interceptors launched several forays into the skies over northwestern Iran, and attempted to intercept some of the many airliners underway between Europe and southern and South-East Asia.*

The gloves were off and the IRIAF F-5 pilots swore revenge. Studying the operations of Iraqi MiG-25s, they concluded that because cities like Tehran, Qom and Esfahan were nearing the end of their endurance and thus incapable of defending themselves, let alone launching ground-to-air attacks, the Iraqis tended to slow down and then descend while returning in an easterly direction in order to save fuel. A slow-flying MiG-25 was a sluggish and practically defenceless target.

After several unsuccessful attempts, a MiG-25 was detected on 4 July 1986 high over Ardabil attempting to catch a passenger aircraft underway over Iran towards Turkey. When it reached Ourumiyeh, two F-5Es were scrambled from TFB.2, flown by Colonel Mohammad Zare-Nejad and Captain Majid Shabani. Zare-Nejad recalled:

> We were on QRA early in the morning, when ordered to scramble. While checking the functionality of my aircraft, I detected a problem and changed the plane, and then took off... The ground control ordered us to climb to 3,600 metres. The sun was not yet completely up and I was guessing about a possible engagement with an enemy intruder when the control ordered me to turn north, and then south. We haven't completed our first turn when controllers called us again, advising that the target was now at our 12 o'clock [straight ahead], range about 20 kilometres and high above us. We engaged afterburners and started to climb, and I advised my wingman to monitor the sky around us.
>
> I sighted the target already seconds later, but didn't recognize it as a MiG-25 because it was still far away. I jettisoned my drop tank to lighten my aircraft and then the controller called to warn me about the type of target. Because I knew that the MiG-25 had a very good radar-warning-receiver and powerful ECM-systems, I decided to keep my radar on stand-by and lock-on only when well within range. My wingman did the same too.
>
> We climbed to 8,800 metres, approached the desired distance unobserved and I locked on my AIM-9Js, but they didn't fire because of technical malfunction. My wingman and me switched to cannons and I fired, and saw a smoke trail from the right wing of the target.

Captain Majid Shabani takes up the story:

> Our ground control – radar officer Capt Hoda, a very good and experienced officer – told us, he wants us to circle around a specific point and then we were to manoeuvre, intercept and shoot down the enemy aircraft while this was returning towards Iraq. We followed his instructions, me always to the right from Colonel Zare-Nejad. We picked up speed and had good acceleration when the intercept started, while the MiG was still some 7,000-8,000ft above us. Then I saw my friend (Zare-Nejad) firing his 20mm cannon and the target emiting smoke. There was an explosion and it started to burn. The passenger plane distanced safely and landed in Turkey.

Although never officially admitting this loss and even deleting it from their official records, the Iraqis subsequently confirmed that their MiG-25 was hit by "a few 20mm shell", which supposedly "caused little damage". Nevertheless, they also confirmed that the IrAF had to write off this MiG, after it made an emergency landing on a forward air strip in northeastern Iraq.†

OPERATION SHAFAGH (VALFAJR-8)

After several years of much-reduced activity, the IRIAF managed to recover many of its capabilities. By late 1985 the number of FMC F-5E/Fs had more than doubled, enabling TFB.2 and TFB.4 to maintain a near-permanent detachment of 10 aircraft at the – still in-complete – TFB.5, in Omidiyeh. The first big operation during this period was Shafagh, undertaken in support of ground forces during the offensive Valfajr-8, which aimed to occupy the Faw Peninsula in southern Iraq, beginning on 9 February 1986.

Following directions it received from the military committee of the presidential office of Iran – headed by Lieutenant-Colonel Abdullah Najafi – the IRIAF planned Operation Shafaqh to last 15 days ("extendable to a month") and make provision for CAS for IRGC ground forces, interdiction strikes against selected targets behind the front-line, provision of air defence by means of Hawk and Rapier SAMs, reinforced by AA guns, and the provision of top cover with by F-4s, F-5s and F-14s. Theoretically, the IRIAF was in good condition to operate accordingly. However, in practice, demands for its involvement in Operation Valfajr-8 meant that it had to withdraw many of its resources from other vital tasks, such as the protection of strategically important installations – foremost the oil-exporting industry – elsewhere in Iran.

Operation Shafagh was initiated on 5 January 1986 when TFB.2 deployed eight F-5Es to Vahdati to replace 10 F-5Es and two F-5Fs deployed to TFB.5. Five days later the Tiger IIs flew the first preparatory strike of this operation, bombing the Ali AB outside Nassiryah and the forward airfield near Umm ol-Qassr used by light aircraft and helicopters of the IrAF. Subsequently, F-5s supported high-flying F-14 CAPs, as in earlier times, and flew dozens of strikes against major enemy HQs in southern Iraq, frequently disrupting their function

---

* Brigadier-General Ahmad Sadik (IrAF, ret.), interview with Tom Cooper, March 2005.

† Brigadier-General Ahmad Sadik (IrAF, ret.), interview with Tom Cooper, March 2005 and a report on the interrogation of 1st Lieutenant Tysir Subhi Ahmad-Ali, an Iraqi MiG-25RBT pilot shot down and captured over Esfahan on 15 February 1987. Curiously, the report: *Analytical Study of Iraqi Aircraft Attrition during the Iran-Iraq War*, prepared by the IrAF Intelligence Directorate in 1992, and provided in full by Brigadier-General Sadik to Tom Cooper, does not mention any such loss.

Javad Mohammadian seen on the tarmac at TFB.2 in 1979. The F-5E behind him, serial 3-7080, was lost in 1980. (Babak Taghvaee Collection)

Colonel Mohammad Zare-Nejad (right) and Captain Majid Shabani (left) and F-5E with 3-7102 serial number (c/n: U1090) at TFB.2 after their successful mission on 4 July 1986. (via Kouros Pashazadeh)

and heightening the chaos caused by the sudden appearance of Iranian ground forces on the Faw Peninsula. Sayed Mohammad Taghi Fazeli recalled a mission marred by technical problems he flew on 1 February 1986:

Mustafa Ardestani led our pair, and we passed south of Bandar-e Khomeyni and then towards Bahmanshir River at a very low alitutde. We followed the flight plan, reached our target without problems and then climbed for bomb release. When I triggered the switch, only the Mk.84 bomb under my centreline hardpoint released: all four M-117s remained struck to their underwing hardpoints. Ardestani noticed my problem and ordered me to pull the emergency t-handle, so I jetissoned remaining weapons and descended back to low altitude, to avoid enemy anti-aircraft fire.

For much of early February, bad weather hampered flying operations and it was only on the 11th of that month that four F-5Es armed with BL.755s and BLU-1Bs attacked the main Iraqi HQ north of Faw, as recalled by Samad-Ali Bala-Zadeh:

I flew as wingman to Ardestani, at very low altitude under clouds. The weather improved after we passed Bandar Khomeyni and approached Faw, but then the skies filled with mushrooms from Iraqi flaks positioned around the Salt Factory in the centre of Peninsula. We approached from the south and then turned to bomb enemy tanks near the factory.

Although flying an average of 20 CAS sorties into one of best defended parts of Iraq, the IRIAF avoided suffering losses due to very careful planning and the employment of loft-bombing. The latter saw the F-5s approaching their targets at a very low altitude, releasing bombs while in a shallow climb from stand-off ranges and then immediately returning to low altitude. Such operations proved very complex to plan and execute because Tiger IIs lacked the necessary automatic systems and pilots had to stick precisely to their flight plans, maintaining specific speed, g-force and climb angles until reaching the release point. Although errors did happen time and again, Iraqi eyewitnesses confirmed the precision of such sorties.

The IrAF did everything possible to improve its defences against loft-bombing attacks. Indeed, on 12 February 1986, newly deployed SA-6s had shot down the F-5E

3-7106 flown by Captain Ghasem Warzdar as it was climbing for release. The pilot ejected safely and became a PoW.

The four F-5Es that attacked an Iraqi divisional HQ north of al-Faw the next day applied the same tactics, but 3-7098 flown by Captain Abulfazl Asad-Zadeh was hit by ZSU-23-4 Shilka self-propelled, radar-controlled anti-aircraft fire, Samad-Ali Bala-Zadeh recalls:

> In reaction to our loft-bombing tactics, the Iraqis put up a true 'firewall' of flak-fire in front of us. We were not able to avoid it because our tactics required extremely precise flying. I entered this firewall, and fired several bursts from my 20mm cannons attempting to suppress and reduce their fire. Then I climbed and released, recovering to low altitude over Bubiyan Island [in Kuwait]. Then an alarm bell ringed, and I noticed that my airspeed indicator was malfunctioning. There was a hole in my windscreen and my wingman's canopy was damaged too. I asked my wingman to land back at TFB.5 together with me, but he was too scared and went on to land at the first opportunity. I landed after him, gauging my speed by dead reckoning. I didn't want to punish him: we were the last pilots at TFB.5 and because of earlier losses and accidents all were in bad moods. I found no motivation in either encouraging them to fly more missions or to punish anybody for failing to provide support.

Ahmad Mehrnia flew with Mustafa Ardestani at the end of the same attack:

> Ardestani and me launched from TFB.5 and approached our target in complete radio silence, though in coordination with five or six other formations. The Iraqis put up a massive volume of flak, and circumstances became tumultuous, causing us to break the radio silence. In front of me I saw the F-5E of Capt Asad-Zadeh pulling up, then suddenly alightning in flame and going down. He was shot down and killed. All of other aircraft received different amounts of damage too. Our pair entered our climb over Arvand Rüd. We released and immediately descended, but by that time even Ardestani's F-5 was damaged. His centreline drop tank was hit and its wreckage hit his left wing upon separating, causing one of bombs not to release. Moments later, his fin and left engine were on fire! Ardestani remained calm: he automatically turned back in direction of Iran, shut down the left engine, and nursed the plane back to TFB.5 at minimal speed and altitude to make a safe emergency landing.

Ardestani concluded:

> ... I was surprised to return safely on one engine. Even more so once I was back on the ground: there was a half-a-metre sized hole in the belly of my F-5 and my left engine was completely destroyed!

Ali Gholami served at the Ra'ad HQ during this operation, and recalled the situation on the battlefields of Faw Peninsula as of mid-February 1986 as follows:

> Our forces crossed the Arvand Rüd and occupied the Faw Peninsula, but Iraqis concentrated nearly all of their army to stop our offensive and counter-attack. Iraqis launched their first major counter-offensive on 16 February and commander of IRGC forces on the Faw, Gen Hemmat, requested support from the IRIAF. However, bad weather prevented us from helping the IRGC. Colonel Baba'ie, an F-14-pilot and the IRIAF representative at the Raad HQ, explained this to Hemmat, but he continued insisting. Eventually, Ardestani volunteered to do the mission: he took off alone and in bad weather, and bombed the enemy forces. But, more was really not possible.

While ground crews were repairing the damaged F-5Es at TFB.5, they were reinforced by four Tiger IIs from TFB.4 on 17 February when Ahmad Mehrnia volunteered to fly another such attack:

> I was the only F-5 pilot at TFB.5 ready to fly in such weather. I passed the Arvand Rüd and then flew into the Iraqi airspace, noticing a number of famous enemy tri-angle positions and many tank shelters below me, all surrounded by flak batteries. The Iraqis obviously thought I would be an Iraqi, and didn't open fire, so I reached the al-Bahar military base, bombed and returned to Omidiyeh unscatched. There I met Mustafa Ardestani, who laughed at me. I asked for reason and he said, 'IRGC forces requested another such strike. They told me you have broken an enemy attack. Al-Bahar base was their CP and when it was hit, they retreated!"

Two days later, four F-5Es from TFB.5 bombed the Iraqi positions on the western side of the Faw Peninsula, as recalled by Javad Mohammadanian:

> We planned that mission the night before, and decided that because of bad weather, we should fly along a different route. I was assigned to fly as wingman to Maj Brijand Beik-Mohammadi, we flew as second pair in the flight led by Maj Manucher Shariati and Capt Vali-Allah Bozorgi. Shariati and Bozrogi launched as first, at 07.30hrs local time in the morning, and we followed ten minutes later. We reached the northern Persian Gulf without any problem, and then turned for Faw, crossing the coast near Qor Abdullah. Then I've heard Shariati on the raido advising his wingman, 'Vali, turn right, I'll turn left, we'll return over the water!' I decided to do the same. When we reached the target, I released bombs but as I was turning left, my plane received a flak hit in the left wing, which caused it to turn right... While bringing my plane back under control, I've heard Shariati calling Bozorgi on the radio, but there was no response. His plane had been shot down while already over the waters of the Persian Gulf. Fishermen later found his body.

After the loss of F-5E 3-7040 and its pilot, the IRIAF decided that the Iraqi air defences over the Faw Peninsula were simply too formidable. Having no means to suppress enemy air defences, the air force decided to fly one final mission into this zone. Four Tiger IIs attacked Iraqi positions on 23 February 1986, but the F-5E serialled 3-7079 – veteran of hundreds of dangerous sorties over Iraq – was shot down. Its pilot, Major Mansour Mohammadi-Azad ejected but hit the ground hard and died in an Iraqi hospital. His body was returned to Iran 17 years later.

Birjand Beik Mohammadi can be seen at left. He played a key role in planning many IRIAF missions during Operation Shafagh. The F-5E in the background is 3-7021, and it remains operational with the 41st TFS.
(Babak Taghvaee Collection)

Major Mansour Mohammadi-Azad was KIA while flying the F-5E 3-7079 during the last IRIAF attack on Iraqi positions on the Faw Peninsula on 23 February 1986.
(Babak Taghvaee Collection)

MOVING TO TFB.7

As mentioned, the IRIAF recognized the need to train new pilots and ground personnel quite early during the war with Iraq. However, for many years it lacked the opportunity and equipment to take the necessary steps to address this issue. The situation only changed once the F-5Bs, stored at Mehrabad, were returned to service, and the first of the overhauled former Ethiopian Freedom Fighters became available in October 1986 – by 1988 this squadron was reinforced by all the surviving RF-5As from the 11th TRS. During that month the aircraft and their crews moved to TFB.7 outside Shiraz and established a new unit, the 71st CCT – replacing an F-14 squadron that was disbanded earlier that year. The first task of the new squadron was to provide advanced training for a group of 20 IRIAF cadets fresh from flight training in Pakistan. Two experienced pilots were qualified as instructors. The unit also served to fly point-defence interceptor sorties for the defence of Shiraz. Further to all this, pilots of the 71st CCT clocked 1,950 hours combat flying time against Iraq by the end of the war.

Meanwhile, after participating in Operation Shafagh, the IRIAF was forced to reduce the activity of its F-5 units again. Henceforth and until the end of the war with Iraq, Iranian Tiger IIs flew only two types of combat sorties: CAPs and strikes deep into Iraq, so-called 'special missions'. In March 1986, the Raad HQ ordered TFB.4 to attack the al-Bahar base again. Four pilots volunteered to fly the mission, being Ardestani, Ghasemi, Yousefi and Chegini. They hit the Iraqis heavily and returned without incident.

The prohibition of flying CAS sorties was temporarily lifted in May 1986 when Iraq launched a local offensive on the border town of Mehran, and Iranian ground forces counterattacked in Operation Karbala-1. Samad-Ali Belazadeh recalled:

> On 1 July I flew a loft-bombing mission against Iraqis near Mehran. I found no manuals for such operations, and did not practice it since the revolution, so Babai'e ordered me to join several other pilots that flew few practice sorties. The procedure was actually very easy, but a small mistake on the part of the pilot resulted in a big mistake and waste of bombs.
> We launched from Vahdati and approached the battlefield at low level. Our and Iraqi lines were very close to each other and we had to be careful not to hit Iranian ground forces. Seven kilometres away from the target, we entered a climb: my wingman released too early, and his bombs hit an empty Iranian trench. Fortunately, nobody was injured. But, my bombs

Captain Vali-Allah Bozorgi was killed while flying the F-5E 3-7040 over Faw in February 1986.
(via Mahmood Sabet-Pasha)

3-7011 in its original colour scheme can be seen at TFB.7 just weeks after the establishment of 71st CCTS. (Babak Taghvaee Collection)

Colonel Jalal Aram (right) commander of 71st CCTS can be seen in front of the squadron building at TFB.7. (Babak Taghvaee Collection)

Abbas Elmi piloted the F-5E that was shot down near Mehran on 2 July 1986. He ejected safely but was captured by Iraqis. (via Mahmood Sabet-Pasha)

war. We turned around the place to re-orient, found our target and dropped our bombs on the pump. The Iraqi flak then hit my plane and I lost one engine, but we recovered safely at Vahdati.

The reinforced Iraqi air defences made such missions extremely risky as on 14 August 1986 when both F-5Es sent to bomb the oil refinery near Suleimaniyah – flown by Captain Yousef Samandarian and Captain Abbas-Ramezani – were shot down. Both pilots ejected safely; Samandarian was captured and Ramezani was rescued by Kurds who returned him to Iran. Samandarian recalled:

I was Deputy CO 41st TFS at that time. When we received the order to attack Suleimaniya, our CO, Colonel Ghorbani, was on sick leave, so I volunteered to fly the mission with Ramezani as my wingman. We forward deployed to TFB.3 and flew our mission from there on the late afternoon of 14 August. Already while approaching our target, we were confronted with a thick firewall of enemy flak fire. Because our aircraft lacked a radar-warning-receiver, and because of the stress caused by enemy flak fire, we failed to see SAMs fired at us and my plane received damage from a near-miss. I lost one engine but released my bombs on targets. Then I lost the other engine too. When my hydraulic pressure dropped to 0, I ejected while underway only some 50-60 metres above the ground. I landed very hard, injuring my spine. Fortunately, three Iraqi soldiers arrested me before local people could get me into their hands ...

EVACUATION OF VAHDATI

On 24 December 1986 the IRGC deployed 100,000 troops to launch Operation Karbala-4, with the intention of breaching enemy fronts east of the second biggest Iraqi city, Basra. With this offensive being undertaken with little cooperation from the regular Iranian military, the IRIAF was slow in reacting. However, Karbala-4 failed before the air force was able to deploy its assets closer to the battlefields and thus no support missions were flown.

The IRGC regrouped and launched a new offensive, Karbala-5, on 9 February 1987, this time in close cooperation with the regular Iranian armed forces. The Iranians managed to breach three Iraqi fronts, destroy several dozen Iraqi armoured vehicles and other heavy

were released on time and hit the enemy trenches.

Nasrollah Erfani and Abbas Elmi flew another such sortie, the next day, but by then the Iraqis have reinforced their air defences and these shot down Elmi's F-5E as this was releasing bombs. He ejected safely but became a prisoner of war. I flew additional such sorties between 4 and 9 July, usually on an F-5F with Colonel Babai'e in the backseat.

On 8 August 1986, Samad-Ali Belazadeh was involved in a special mission against targets deep inside Iraq:

We attacked the al-Amara oil pump. Arriving over that city, I found it much bigger then it had been during the first year of the

Captain Yousef Samandarian. (via Sarah Naderi)

armament, and capture 2,385 Iraqi soldiers.

The Tiger IIs from TFB.4 were involved in this operation from the start. Forward deployed to TFB.5, they primarily flew interdiction strikes against major Iraqi HQs. They flew some CAPs too, but due to the small number of available F-5s, most of these missions were flown by a single aircraft. Unsurprisingly, when Captain Hamid Barzegari Nasr-Abadi was scrambled to intercept two Iraqi Mirage F.1s underway to Lake Ourumiyeh, he was ambushed, shot down, and killed on 17 February 1987.

With Karbala-5 turning into one of the largest battles of the war, TFB.4 intensified its operations, repeatedly hitting various Iraqi command centres. These caused such significant losses and problems for Iraq that the IrAF high command eventually ordered an all-out attack on Vahdati AB on 13 April 1987. This operation involved nearly 100 Iraqi aircraft, primarily MiG-23BNs and Su-22s, which reached their target in five waves. Although failing to cause any serious damage to the runway, fortified installations or HASs, their bombs demolished the fire department building, killing several firefighters; it damaged the F-5 maintenance hangar and the maintenance hangar for the Beech F.33 Bonanca liaison aircraft. Also damaged were two F-5Es, one deHavilland Canada L-20B light transport and two F.33Cs. Worst of all, many Iraqi bombs fell on nearby apartment buildings, killing dozens of civilians. After this tragedy the IRIAF was left with little choice but to evacuate TFB.4, leaving only four F-5Es. All operational aircraft, most personnel and all related civilians were withdrawn to TFB.7 and TFB.8.

LAST SPECIAL MISSIONS
During the last year of the Iran-Iraq War, the surviving IRIAF F-5s were limited to flying CAPs and providing support to secondary operations along the central and northern frontlines with Iraq. In August 1987 they supported the Iranian army by combating a concentration of 15 Iraqi army brigades in the Maimak area – Operation Nasr-6 – primarily through the provision of CASs and top cover for the IRIAA helicopters. The IRIAF suffered one loss during this offensive – on 6 August 1987 the F-5F 3-7173 received a hit from friendly ZU-23 flak while flying visual reconnaissance over Sardasht. The shell exploded inside the rear cockpit of the aircraft, killing Colonel Baba'ie. The pilot, Colonel Naderi (then CO TFB.2) executed a safe emergency landing in Tabriz.

Later that month TFB.2 launched three successful strikes on the Dukan Dam but had two of its F-5Es damaged by enemy air defences on 31 August. Captains Belazadeh and Dariush-Zare managed to nurse their aircraft back to base and make safe emergency landings. Later the same day, the Tiger II units from TFB.4 were less lucky when the F-5E flown by Captain Ali-Asghar Behniya was shot down; the pilot was killed although the exact circumstances of his death are unclear.

In March 1988 the Iranians launched their last major offensive of the war, Operation Valfajr-10. This offensive was avidly supported by F-5Es of the 22nd TFS, which conducted dozens of CAS sorties from TFB.3. The surprised Iraqis fled the battlefield but Baghdad was prompted into ordering the IrAF to launch one of the most expansive attacks with chemical weapons during the war. In a series of strikes against the town of Halabcheh, Iraqi chemical weapons killed more than 5,000 civilians and several dozen Iranian soldiers, while wounding more than 5,000.

During the same month the IrAF continued bombing Iranian towns along the border, thus TFB.2 exploited every opportunity to strike back. By the end of March, the IRIAF F-5Es repeatedly hit selected targets in the towns of Qaladiza and Erbil.

OPERATION MERSAD
In July 1988 Ayatollah Khomeini finally granted permission to his government in Tehran to accept a UN-negotiated ceasefire with Iraq, thus ending the war. Generally, this ceasefire was accepted by both sides. However, the Iraqis did make a final attempt at taking the Iranians by surprise. During the 1980s, they harboured the terrorist group Mujaheddin-e-Khalq (MEK/MKO), which largely consisted of extreme leftist post-revolution Iranian refugees. The MEK/MKO launched a number of terrorist attacks inside Iran, targeting members of the military and security forces, but also civilians. By 1987 Iraq had established two bases where about 10,000 of these militants were concentrated, trained and armed. Once this force was ready, Baghdad waited for an opportunity to unleash it. The moment came six days before the ceasefire.

The original plan for this operation – codenamed Eternal Light (Forough-e-Javidan) – envisaged a massive IrAF attack on TFB.2, TFB.3 and TFB.4 in order to paralyze the IRIAF. The MEK/MKO – meanwhile equipped with armoured cars and artillery provided by Iraq – was then to advance across the border and on the provincial capital of Kermanshah in northwestern Iran. Although the Iraqis did not launch their planned attacks on IRIAF air bases, the offensive caught the Iranians by surprise and the terrorists advanced nearly 145 kilometres into Iran before encountering resistance from local Kurdish militias which slowed them down, buying time for a counter-attack by the Iranian military. Organized under the codename Operation Mersad, this counter-attack received powerful support from the

IRIAF which deployed all of the 22nd and 41st TFS F-5Es and all F-5A/Bs of the newly-established 72nd TFS into counter-attacks. These found the mechanized columns of the MEK/MKO exposed in the open, unprotected by the IrAF and in possession of only the bare minimum of air defence weapons. After providing covering support for the C-130 Hercules transports that dropped the Iranian army paratroopers at the end of the enemy column, Iranian Tiger IIs bombed, rocketed and strafed the enemy, in turn distracting their attention from the Bell AH-1J Cobra attack helicopters of the IRIAA that then knocked out all the Brazilian-made Cascavel armoured cars operated by the terrorists. Finally, Iranian ground troops overran the enemy, killing more than 4,500 and capturing at least 400. Samad-Ali Belizadeh was serving at TFB.2 as of 23 July 1988:

> Despite accepting the Resolution 598 on 18 July, the Iraqis and the terrorists have invaded Iran again. The Iraqis attacked in direction of Khorramshar, to divert our attention from terrorist attack on Kermanshah. We received the order to forward deploy to TFB.5, quickly. Together with me were Seyed Mohammad Taghi Fazeli, Mohammad-Hossein Darabi and Ali Nasiri-Vatan. We arrived at Omidiyeh only to find it nearly deserted. There was no activity. I ordered the ground crews to re-open the CP and the ammunition depot, but they told me they have no permission to do that, and were not permitted to arm our F-5s. In fact, they were not informed about our mission. I broke the doors of both compounds and then ordered the technicians to arm our aircraft. That was illegal, but there was no other choice. Once ready, I lead my formation flying an F-5F with Darabi in the rear cockpit. We bombed Iraqi tanks, returned to re-arm and then flew two more sorties that day, and seven in the following days. Eventually, the Iraqis were forced to withdraw.

Chapter three
STRUGGLE FOR SURVIVAL

During the war with Iraq, the IRIAF lost 55 F-5 pilots (46 of them KIA), and was forced to write off a total of 77 F-5Es, six F-5Fs, one RF-5A and one F-5B. In addition, 10 badly damaged F-5Es and two F-5Fs were in need of extensive repairs; the air force only had 36 operational F-5Es, 18 F-5Fs, 10 RF-5As and 11 F-5Bs in July 1988. This dire state of the fleet was one of the major reasons why the IRIAF decided to purchase as many Ethiopian F-5s, despite their poor condition, as possible. By 1990, five F-5Es, eight F-5As and one ex-Ethiopian F-5B were completely refurbished and in service. This meagre fleet of survivors was operated by six squadrons, including the 21st and 22nd TFS at TFB.2, the 41st and 42nd TFS at TFB.4 and the 71st CCTS and the 72nd TFS at TFB.7.

During the late 1980s Tehran launched several attempts to acquire aircraft that could replace its battered F-5s. The IRGC ordered Shenyang F-7 fighters from China and MiG-21s from East Germany and there were negotiations with the communist government of Romania over a possible acquisition of IAR-93 Orao fighter bombers, manufactured in cooperation with Yugoslavia. However, the Romanian government was overturned before any agreement was reached; only two former East German MiGs had reached Iran before that country was reunited with its western counterpart; and the F-7s proved a maintenance nightmare which the IRGC was unable to operate. Precious time was lost and it was only in 1989 that the Iranian government entered negotiations with Moscow, intending to purchase around 100 combat aircraft in order to replenish the depleted IRIAF stocks. Although the Soviets agreed to deliver, the USSR fell into disarray soon afterward and a much-weakened Russian Federation subsequently found itself under fierce US pressure. This and Iranian financial difficulties resulted in the delivery of relatively small numbers of MiG-29 interceptors and Su-24MK fighter bombers in 1990 and 1991. As such, the workhorse Northrop F-5s had to continue serving with the IRIAF, which in turn meant that the air force had to find the ways to adapt them for further service.

Furthermore, despite the ceasefire with Iraq, and although defeating the MEK/MKO, Iran found itself under newly emerging threats. Preoccupied with its border with Iraq and that war, the government of Iran had neglected the security of its eastern borders for much of the 1980s. This opened the country to myriad activities by various Afghan and Pakistani drug-trafficking gangs. Several of these developed strong paramilitary structures and even brought significant parts of Iranian territory under their control. As a result, whatever aircraft were available and operational had to continue serving and flying new combat missions.

Indeed, the F-5s from TFB.4 and TFB.7 became involved in operations against such drug traffickers in January 1989 when one F-5F, four F-5Es, two F-5As and two F-5Bs were deployed to Zahedan IAP. After conducting several visual reconnaissance missions in order to get accustomed to the local terrain and find suitable targets, their pilots began flying attack sorties on the 9th and 10th of the same month. However, after local authorities complained that their operations would scare civilians, the IRIAF pilots were prohibited from deploying their weapons. During one of the final missions from Zahedan, the F-5F piloted by Parviz Nasri and Tehrani Moghaddam with the F-5E (probably serial 3-7144 from 72nd TFS) piloted by Bahman Akbari, were conducting a visual surveillance sortie over the mountains east of Zahedan when an awful and unnecessary accident occurred. Both flew at low level and high speed and then the pilots started racing. The F-5E graunched the ground, ingesting dirt into the engine, resulting in its failure. Akbari attempted an emergency landing on the Kurband road but nearly collided with a civilian car. He ejected. Akbari injured his spine and the aircraft suffered extensive damage to the landing gear and nose section, and required substantial repairs to return to service.

ATTACKS ON CAMP ASHRAF

Although severely defeated during the Operation Mersad, the survivors of the MEK/MKO gathered in Iraq again and continued receiving support from the Iraqi government. Following the Iraqi defeat at the hands of the US coalition that liberated Kuwait in March 1991, the Kurds in northern Iraq launched an uprising. The government in Baghdad deployed the MEK/MKO to defuse

F-5E serialled 3-7059 (c/n: U1047) and F-5F serialled 3-7159 (c/n: Z1006) are seen in 1993 above Abdanan heights located in northwest Dezful. Both are armed with AIM-9J missiles for photo-shooting. (Babak Taghvaee Collection)

the situation. As an off-shoot to this, the terrorists launched a new advance into Iran, and temporarily captured the Morvarid Heights inside the Iranian Kermanshah Province on 1 April 1991, massacring hundreds of Iranian-Kurdish civilians in the process.

On the morning of 5 April the IRIAF reacted by launching nine F-4Es from TFB.3 to hit Camp Ashraf, the main MEK/MKO base about 80 kilometres inside Iraq and 28 kilometres north of the town of Khalis. Five minutes later, nine F-5Es from TFB.4 followed suit. The crew of one of the Phantoms (serial 3-6688) failed to execute its pop-up manoeuvre correctly and was forced to eject – both pilots were captured by the MEK/MKO and handed over to the Iraqis.

During the following years Turkey became involved in a war against the insurgents of the Kurdish Workers Party, supported by Iraq and its military. It launched several operations along the border with Iran. F-4 Phantoms of the Turkish Air Force violated Iranian airspace on several occasions and were repeatedly warned off but the IRIAF never attempted to intercept them – the F-5Es from TFB.2 were simply rendered ineffective against the much faster Turkish Phantoms, usually escorted by General Dynamics (later Lockheed) F-16C Fighting Falcons. Correspondingly, the Iranian Air Force decided to reinforce Tabriz AB through the deployment of MiG-29s, recently acquired from the former Soviet Union. This original temporary deployment became permanent and eventually the decision was made to transfer all the F-5Es of the 22nd TFS to the 21st TFS and convert the 22nd TFS later to MiG-29s.

Meanwhile, by 1994 the MEK/MKO was launching regular suicide attacks into Iran, assassinating a number of civilian and military officials. The IRIAF was tasked with flying another strike against Camp Ashraf. This little-known mission was flown by one F-5F and three F-5Es from TFB.2 on 9 November 1994. Sixteen Mk.82SE bombs were delivered on target with no damage to the involved aircraft or their crews; their attack was successful, but because this mission was conducted inside the US–British-maintained no-fly zone over northern Iraq, it prompted a scramble of 20 McDonnell Douglas (later Boeing) F-15 and F-16 fighters of the US Air Force from bases in Turkey. TFB.2 was ordered to fly another attack on Camp Ashraf in the summer 1995, but that mission was cancelled due to bad weather.

TENSIONS WITH AFGHANISTAN

Except for becoming involved in operations against the MEK/MKO terrorists, the F-5Es from TFB.2 were frequently tasked with forward deploying to Mashhad IAP in northeastern Iran during the 1990s. In this way they became involved in what nearly resulted in another full-scale war.

During the mid-1990s, the never-ending civil war in Afghanistan intensified as a result of the emergence of the Taliban militia – established and administered by the Pakistanis with strong financial support from Saudi Arabia. The Taliban consisted of militant Sunni Wahhabism and the government of Iran – burdened with the influx of tens of thousands of Afghan refugees due to the Taliban's imposition of tight Sharia laws on the daily lives of Afghan civilians, who now found themselves in the crossfire of a full-scale civil war between the Taliban and Afghanistan's Northern Alliance – became involved by providing aid and supplies to at least two Afghan groups fighting against them (the Taliban) to reduce attacks on eastern Iranian cities and assist in curbing drug trafficking. These included the Jamiat-e-Islami Party headed by Ahmad Shah Massoud and the lesser-known Hezb-e-Wahadat Party.

In reaction to the emergence of the Taliban and their bloody campaign that swept across the country seizing and occupying most of the eastern, southern and central Afghanistan in 1995–1996. Ahmad Shah Massoud and General Abdul Rashid Dostum created the coalition named the United Front (also known as the Northern Alliance UF/NA) but by the end of 1996 they had been forced into the north and northeast of Afganistan while the Taliban held the rest of the country in its vice-like grip. Although it controlled only about 30 percent of the country, the UF/NA was internationally recognized as the government of Afghanistan.

While often described as a disorganized rag tag militia by the West, as a result of support from the Afghan office of the Pakistani Inter-Service Intelligence Agency (ISI), the Taliban established a well-organized military. This included a small but relatively well-equipped and skilfully operated air force, the Islamic Emirate of Afghanistan Air Force (IEAAF). Among others, the IEAAF is known to have had at least five operational Aero L-39C Albatros jet trainers, seven MiG-21 interceptors, and up to ten Su-20M and Su-22M-4K fighter bombers. These aircraft flew their first attacks on UF/NA strongholds in early 1995 and by June that year had already flown combat air patrols in an attempt to establish control of Afghan airspace. Their primary task was to intercept helicopters and transport aircraft chartered by foreign powers – including Iran and the Russian Federation – operated by the UF/NA and it allies to fly supplies to UF/NA-held areas. On 14 June 1995 two IEAAF MiG-21s intercepted a pair of Mi-17 helicopters carrying supplies for Massoud's forces. They shot down one with cannon fire and forced the other to crash. On 3 August 1995 they intercepted a Russian Ilyushin Il-76 transport that was underway with supplies for Massoud and forced it to land at Qandahar airport. The IEAAF was especially active during the Taliban advance on Herat in the second half of 1995 when it managed to cause significant losses to General Dostum's militia. Nevertheless, it too suffered heavy losses, including four MiG-21s and three Mi-8 helicopters that were shot down with the loss of almost their entire crews.[*]

The IRIAF became involved in the Afghan civil war in January 1996 when C-130s from TFB.7 began flying at least six supply missions to Mazar-e-Sharif airport a month, carrying food and medicine to airfields held by Massoud's forces. With the help of these supplies, the UF/NA managed to temporarily halt the Taliban advance on Kabul, the Afghan capital. By that time, the IEAAF only had two airworthy MiG-21s left and they were deployed to deliberately violate Iranian airspace. Taliban ground forces began providing support to drug smugglers trafficking via Iran to Turkey and Europe. After the Saudis, money from heroin and opium trafficking was the second-largest source of income for the Taliban.

The IRIAF reacted by deploying nine F-5Es and three F-5Fs to Mashhad and establishing Tactical Air Base 14 or Imam Reza (TAB.14) at that airport. Correspondingly, the F-5s detached to TAB.14 were organized into the 141st TFS. Soon afterward four Tiger IIs from this unit were redeployed to Khour airport outside Birjand – 382 kilometres south of Mashhad – where TAB.12 came

into being. Usually armed with two AIM-9Js, the F-5s at these two air bases stood at QRA duty and were scrambled a number of times in reaction to the appearance of Taliban-operated MiG-21s and Su-22s.

In early 1997 the Taliban attacked the positions of the Dostum's militia and alomost completely destroyed it, forcing most survivors to flee across the border to Afghanistan's neighbours. Some of Dostum's officers even defected to the Taliban, including one pilot that 'delivered' a Mi-17 helicopter to the IEAAF. By the summer of 1997 the Taliban turned their attention to the border with Iran, threatening to attack the Mashhad and Khorasan provinces. In reaction, the Iranians deployed their army and IRGC forces along the border, while the 141st TFS was reinforced by F-5Es from TFB.4, followed by three former Iraqi Mirage F.1BQs and seven Mirage F.1EQ-5/6 interceptors redeployed from TFB.3.[†] Eventually, the French-built fighters were used to establish another new unit, the 142nd TFS.

Despite a few artillery exchanges and the F-5s flying some ground attack sorties – primarily against drug traffickers – and although an outbreak of open hostilities seemed probable, tensions dissipated and the IRIAF was able to return to routine peacetime operations in 1998.

Indeed, the activity and presence of Iranian F-5s at Mashhad was subsequently curtailed. The threat of the Taliban had, for the most part, evaporated by late 2002 after the Iranian-supported and US-led coalition invaded Afghanistan. With many former Iraqi Mirages out of service due to lack of spares, and with its F-5 fleet in bad condition, the IRIAF deactivated the 142nd TFS – Mirages were stored at Mashhad, while F-5s returned to their parent units at TFB.2 and TFB.4. TAB.14 remained an active IRIAF outpost, but was renamed Habibi Air Base in commemoration of Colonel Nasser Habibi Zoham, its deputy of operations killed in a Mirage F.1EQ-5 accident on 5 July 2001. TAB.12 was subsequently deactivated and F-5s ceased deploying there.

The position of TAB.14 experienced a change prompted by a change in US policy toward Iran in 2003. While clandestinely cooperating with Tehran during the invasions of Afghanistan and Iraq, the administration of US President George W. Bush subsequently declared Iran a member of the Axis of Evil and indirectly threatened it with an invasion. The IRIAF reactivated the 141st TFS and had at least eight F-5Es – often reinforced by F-4s from the 91st TFS – deployed at Mashhad during the following years.

TENSIONS WITH AZERBAIJAN

Little is known about Iran's stressed relationship with Azerbaijan. In mid-2001 Iranian F-5s almost got themselves involved in another war. On 21 July SS *Geophysic-3*, operated by a BP Consortium on behalf of of the Republic of Azerbaijan, entered Iranian territorial waters in the Caspian Sea. Once there, the ship began exploring the Iranian oil and gas fields of Sharg, Alov and Araz. Soon after this violation, sailors of the Azerbaijani navy arrived to collect buoys demarcating the territorial waters of the two countries and reposition

---

[*] Indeed, one of the two IEAAF Mi8s known to have been shot down by ground fire on 12 November 1995, carried the Taliban leader, Mullah Omar. Omar was however one of few survivors of that crash.

[†] The Mirages in queston were evacuated to Iran by the Iraqi Air Force in January 1991, during the latter's war with Kuwait. Although originally agreeing with Baghdad to safeguard IrAF aircraft, the Iranian government eventually decided to impound and not repatriate these aircraft, but keep them in the name of reparations for the Iraqi aggression of 1980. Since the Iraqis flew their Mirages to Iran without any armament, the IRIAF was forced to improvize. Correspondingly, prior to their deployment to TAB.14 they have received LAU-7A missile launchers taken from F-14s and were armed with AIM-9J Sidewinders.

Six fully mission-capable F-5Es armed with AIM-9Js were on 24-hour standby, or Quick Reaction Alert, at the IRIAF's forward air station of Mashhad (previously TFB.14) to defend Iran's northeastern airspace. (Photo by Babak Taghvaee)

them further south. The Iranian navy reacted by deploying the corvette IRINS *Hamzeh*, the crew of which removed all the displaced buoys and repositioned them to their original position. By August 2001 Lockheed P-3F Orion maritime patrol aircraft of the IRIAF were flying several patrols over the Caspian Sea. One of them was intercepted by two Azerbaijani MiG-25s. The P-3F's flight crew was ordered to land in Baku. Foxbat pilots, armed with only R-60MK short-range AAMs, reacted quickly and two F-14As locked on to the MiG-25s forcing them to leave the area.

Tehran was under immense pressure, firstly from the US, and secondly it considered itself involved in an undeclared war imposed on it by Israel – in 2001 Israel had accused the Azeri regime of supporting Palestinian terrorists by neglecting to attend to the activities of Hizb ut-Tahrir;* Israel prepared their navy to occupy Iranian territorial waters and oil regions – and thirdly the actions of the Azerbaijani air force, navy and BP were not minor incidents. Iranian intelligence had detected lively cooperation between Israeli intelligence and the Azerbaijani military and security apparatus. Because of US and Israeli threats, Tehran considered the Azerbaijani actions as a possible provocation instigated to draw Iran into a war.

Taking nothing for granted, the IRIAF F-5Es, MiG-29s and F-14s began flying combat air patrols over the Caspian Sea. Their pilots

were ordered to open fire – and shoot down – any Azerbaijani aircraft they encountered. Indeed, at least one case is known in August of that year, in which a pair of IRIAF Tomcats forced two Azerbaijani interceptors into a hasty retreat toward Baku – albeit without opening fire. Simultaneously, the IRIAF high command developed several contingency plans; one of which included the deployment of ten Sukhoi Su-24MK and ten F-4E Phantoms to TFB.2, from where they would conduct offensive operations against the Azerbaijani military in cooperation with locally-based F-5Es and MiG-29s.

Eventually, the much weaker Azerbaijani military backtracked, averting a war. Even so, the IRIAF interceptors flew 108 CAPs over the Caspian Sea during the 18 days of that crisis.

Iranian F-5 crews from TFB.4 experienced similar anxious moments during the US–British-led invasion of Iraq in 2003 when they were scrambled 59 times in reaction to foreign aircraft violating their airspace.

PROJECT SIMOURGH

The IRIAF requirement to restart the training of new pilots and establish the 71st CCTS, in October 1986, resulted in the need to re-equip the unit with more advanced aircraft, or at least increase the number of F-5B trainers in its service and modernize them. Finding no other solution, the IRIAF finally requested the Iranian Aircraft Manufacturing Company (IAMI) to solve the problem.

The IAMI came into being as a result of an international tender for the establishment of a helicopter manufacturing industry, won by the Bell Company. The resulting factories and workshops were completed to 11 percent when the revolution came and the new government stopped further work. However, by that time all the necessary know-how, construction plans, machinery and equipment had already been delivered to Iran. In 1983, the board of directors of the Iranian Defence Industries Organization (DIO) decided to complete the construction according to the pre-revolutionary plan, and by 1986, the IAMI was already running series production of the Ababil UAV.

The major IAMI works were completed in 1988 and the company initially concentrated on manufacturing engines for UAVs and tail booms for Bell 214A and AH-1J helicopters damaged during the war with Iraq, when the DIO and the IRIAF contracted it with the conversion of 12 F-5As and RF-5As into two-seat conversion-trainers.

With some help from the Pakistan Aeronautical Complex, the IAMI used the RF-5A 2-7208 as a prototype and this made its first flight in 1989, under the designation Simourgh. Re-serialled 3-7015, it was delivered to the 71st CCTS in 1990.

By that time, the IAMI had already launched series production of that new type, essentially similar to Northrop's T-38 and F-5B, attempting to roll out two aircraft per year. A lack of the necessary tools and machinery necessary for shaping large parts of the structure and panels for the forward fuselage slowed the process down considerably. Production of new intakes, pitot tube, forward landing gear and a new windshield (and its frame) proved to be less of a problem and were solved with the help of some reverse engineering. The required instrumentation and wiring, ejection seats, hydraulic system, liquid oxygen supply, radios and various minor parts were secured with a little help from black market goods and the IRIAF's limited spare parts stocks. Therefore, the sixth Simourgh entered service with the 85th CCTS in 2000; thus ending the work on the

---

* For years Armenia and Azerbaijan were at war over a border dispute in the Nagorno-Karabakh region. The Azerbi government was helping the Turks, supported by Pan-Islamist terrorist organizations and militias, to fight and massacre Christian defenders of Armenian villages. One of the Pan-Islamic terrorist organizations was Hizb ut-Tahrir.

3-7015 was the first IAMI-manufactured F-5B Simourgh. This aircraft was made from RF-5A serialled 2-7208 (c/n: RF1008). It is still operational with the 43rd CCTS/ TTS at TFB.4 Vahdati. (Photo by Babak Taghvaee)

This unique photo shows 3-7015 after its maiden flight at TFB.8. Note the domestically manufactured forward section, painted in yellow zinc-chromate primer colour while its aft section is still in Asia Minor II colours. The number 1 in the circle stands for the designation of TFB.1, from the time the planes served with the 11th TRS. The windscreen frame and canopy were obtained from Vietnamese stocks, as can be seen by their colour. (Babak Taghvaee Collection)

The fifth Simourgh was made from RF-5A serialled 2-7205 which was still on the vertical fin of the aircraft when this photo was taken. This aircraft would later become 3-7019. (Babak Taghvaee Collection)

The F-5A with serial 2-7252 is a former Ethiopian machine in IRIAF service. It was restored by the Mehrabad Overhaul Centre and returned to service in 2011 when this photo was taken. (photo by Babak Taghvaee)

first batch which was equipped with Martin-Baker IR10LF ejection seats, 50 of which were purchased in 1978 for installation into F-5Bs and RF-5As.

The limited number of such seats and lack of suitable navigational platforms forced the IAMI to scrounge for equivalents when it was contracted to manufacture a second batch of Simourghs in 2006. The solution was found through the installation of Russian-made Zvezda K-36DM ejection seats which were installed in aircraft with serials 3-7021 to 3-7025 (the latter was previously the RF-5A with serial number 2-7212), manufactured between 2007 and 2009.

Since the conversion of Simourghs proceeded at a relatively slow pace, the next project initiated by the IRIAF related to the improvement of the condition of the F-5As and RF-5As in service with the 71st CCTS. By 1990 all the aircraft of the latter variant had lost their reconnaissance capability – although related equipment was still in place, all technicians qualified to maintain it had left the service. Over the course of several months the ground personnel of this unit overhauled the RF-5A 2-7203 in cooperation with the SSJD (Self-Sufficiency Jihad Division), making it operational as a reconnaissance platform again, and the plane re-entered service at Shiraz in 1991.

In 1993, the 71st CCTS suffered a catastrophic loss of two F-5Bs and their crews when 3-7004 and 3-7008 flew into a hill on the Kako gunnery range. Six months later, the 71st CCTS was disbanded and all its aircraft (including five F-5As, seven RF-5As, six F-5Bs and two Simourghs) and crew were transferred to TFB.8, where they established the 85th CCTS with the role of training future pilots for F-14A Tomcats.

PROJECT AZARAKHSH (LIGHTNING)

As described earlier, the Iranian defence sector became capable of manufacturing spares and running complex repairs on all aircraft operated by the air force well before the revolution of 1979. Deliveries of all the necessary technical documentation and material specifications, as well as machinery to the IIAF resulted in the establishment of an F-5 Maintenance Centre at TFB.1. These workshops ran production tests, turning out 40 dummy F-5s that were used as decoys at TFB.2 and TFB.4, before being sold for scrap in 1974 and 1975.

The F-5 Maintenance Centre at Mehrabad was closed after the revolution and its equipment was left to decay. It was only once Iraq invaded Iran that the IRIAF authorities realized the importance of this facility. In late 1980 they therefore scrambled to find all the related documentation and relaunch at least the production of sheet metal spares for F-5s and even F-4s.

One of the first F-5Es restored with the help of this facility was 3-7079, damaged by Iraqi 57mm anti-aircraft flak while flown by Colonel Mohammad Daneshpour in an attack on Dukan Dam on 5 October 1980. The plane had its fin, rudder, right engine and exhaust nozzles badly damaged and was in need of complete rebuilding – completed in 1983. The F-5E 3-7090, badly damaged in November 1980, was the second aircraft rebuilt at this facility.

In 1986, the Maintenance Centre was officially reopened under the designation Owj Complex and the following year its engineers launched an attempt to manufacture the fuselage structure for 30 F-5Es. Thus Project Azarakhsh came into being.

Initial work on this project was actually related to the rebuilding of badly damaged F-5Es with serials 3-7034, 3-7066, 3-7083 and 3-7090. While 3-7066 was in exceptionally bad condition, some of its parts were used to rebuild 3-7083, and eventually at least three restored Tiger IIs were returned to service with TFB.2. However, the Owj Complex initially lacked the machinery necessary to manufacture major structural parts of the F-5; despite success with the rebuilding of damaged aircraft, it failed to produce new ones. It took the IRIAF five years to find and obtain the advanced casting and press machines necessary for the production of spares at the desired quality. The machines in question were obtained from South Africa, and arrived with a group of engineers and metallurgists hired to teach Iranians how to operate these systems.

Using the wreck of 3-7066, pieces obtained from 11 unserviceable F-5Es purchased from Vietnam, and spares from its own production, the Owj Complex eventually managed to 'manufacture' a new aircraft. Thus came into being the first F-5E Azarakhsh, serialled 3-7301, which made its maiden flight in September 1997.

Work on the second Azarakhsh proved more complex and was only completed in 2000, but the resulting aircraft – serial 3-7302 – was also wired for Chinese-made PL-7 AAMs.

PROJECT SAEGHE-80 (THUNDERBOLT-80)

Parallel to work on Azarakhsh and – later on – the SR.II – the Owj Complex employed the two best Iranian aerospace engineers to launch another F-5-related project with the intention of improving the aircraft's aerodynamic capabilities. This resulted in one of the boldest modifications ever introduced on the type – the Saeqeh-80, which is an F-5E variant with two vertical stabilizers.

The necessary research and development was undertaken in cooperation with the IRIAF's Sattari Air University during the mid-1990s and proceeded slowly due to poor management and a lack of even the most basic equipment, such as a wind tunnel. The team working on Saeqeh-80 received material support from the DIO and various private contractors as well as from the IRIAF, which provided one F-5E for conversion to the prototype.

The resulting design incorporated a cubical instead of a curved intake, a new radome with displaced pitot tube, no wingtip missile launchers, one M39 cannon, the IFF system and the TACAN platform – all in order to reduce the overall weight. After 18 months of work, the prototype – serialled S.110-001 – was ready for ground testing and painted overall in light blue with the Iranian flag along the nose section. After performing ten ground runs the plane was flown for the first time on 7 February 2004, usually accompanied by Azarakhsh 3-7302.

The first and second Simorghs were painted white overall, the colours of the Iranian flag since being associated with this type. Not all Simourghs were painted that way though, 3-7017 and 3-7018 retained their Asia Minor II camouflage colour when they were delivered to 85th CCTS. 3-7018 (the aircraft in this photo) is now grounded because of safety isues and a lack of spare parts at Vahdati AB. (Babak Taghvaee Collection)

Flight testing revealed that the re-design of the nose and intakes had adverse effects on the aircraft's manoeuvrabilty. Nevertheless, the IRIAF requested the Owj to prepare the second and third Saeghe and assigned the Azarakhsh 3-7302 and the F-5E 3-7060 to it for that purpose. This time, the engineers didn't change anything regarding the aerodynamic surfaces, they only installed two fins instead of one. The resulting Saegehs S.110-002 and S.110-003 made their first flights in June 2007 and were unveiled to the public a few weeks later. Meanwhile, the Owj began the conversion of another airframe, the former Vietnamese F-5E with serial 73-00873. However, in August 2006, top Iranian clerical leadership made the decision to transfer the entire project – including most of the involved engineers – from the Owj Complex to the IAMI. Ever

2-7250 is the oldest F-5 in IRIAF service. It flew 50 hours before being grounded and used for spares just four months after its restoration in 1992. It was restored again by the Mehrabad Overhaul Center in 2008 and made its first FCF on 8 October 2011. It has served with the 43rd CCTS since and is the best F-5A available for gunnery training. (Photo by Babak Taghvaee)

since, much incorrect information on this project has been released, often including obvious cases of 'photoshopping'. While supposedly launched with the aim of deceiving Western intelligence services, the (mis)information in question caused plenty of controversy and brought an amount of shame on Iran.

The IAMI converted another Saeghe between 2007 and 2008, by which time the entire fleet was reserialled in range 3-7366 to 3-7369. Two additional aircraft followed in 2009 and 2010, although the delivery of the 3-7371 was delayed due to the temporary unavailability of J-85GE-21 engines. Far more damaging was the fact that, despite the original contract from 2003 stipulating deliveries of Saeghes equipped to SR.II standard, the IAMI was only manufacturing 'twin-tailed F-5Es', with their original avionics installed. This resulted in the IRIAF deputy of operations refusing to deliver any further F-5Es to the IAMI for conversion. Work on the seventh Saeghe (serial 3-7372) remained incomplete.

After the reduction of Owj Complex activities, the company-used surplus parts of a former US Navy F-5E to construct this replica in colours of US Navy aircraft until 2006. It eventually ended at the Holy Defence Musuem in Tehran in 2011. (Photo by Babak Taghvaee)

TWIN-SEAT SAEGHES

Without the availability of any twin-seat Saeghe versions, the training of future Saeghe pilots would be costly and difficult. In 2009, the Saeghe squadron was formed and for first time, the IRIAF HQ realized the necessity of having a training version of the Saeghe. The flying characteristics of the Saeghe-80 were similar to its predecessor, the F-5E, but several elements such as the effects of the control surfaces on the aircraft movement around its longitudinal axis (roll axis) demanded at least type-transition training on the aircraft for any F-5 pilot who wanted to become a Saeghe pilot.

In late 2009 the IRIAF's Owj Complex initiated a project named Saeghe-90. It was later renamed Saeghe-II and concerned the installation of the twin vertical Saeghe stabilizers of on F-5Fs.

FIRST SAEGHE.II IS BORN

The Owj Complex delivered an F-5F airframe to the IAMI/HESA to be used as the platform for the first Saeghe.II. The F-5F in question was 3-7180 (c/n Z1027), a former 4th TFB Vahdati aircraft. The reason behind its reassignment to storage in the Owj Complex was as a result of an accident in 2000.

On 21 October 2000, during one of its engine run-ups, one of the technicians mistakenly jettisoned the aircraft canopies. The aircraft boat tail, vertical

Owj Complex staff and personnel were devoted to the Golden Crown aerobatic display team. Its mechanics wore work suits similar to the Golden Crown display team mechanics. They painted the first Azarakhsh (3-7301) in very similar colours to those of the Golden Crown team. Of course, the aircraft was delivered to the IRIAF repainted in the Asia Minor II camouflage pattern. (Babak Taghvaee Collection)

Two of at least 11 former Vietnamese F-5Es acquired by Iran. Most of them were used as the basis for various of Azarakhsh jets, while their remnants were later utilized as decoys. (Photos by Babak Taghvaee)

and horizontal stabilizers were damaged by the canopies. After the accident the F-5F was withdrawn from service and cannibalized for parts. After three years it had no valuable parts left on its airframe.

In 2005 the airframe was handed to the Owj Complex for restoration. The airframe structure and skin were repaired by their technicians and engineers. But due to a lack of vital parts, including its ejection seats which had been destroyed in the accident, it was left in the complex's storage.

The IAMI experts spent two years completing the main airframe of the aircraft. Several hundred metres of wiring were changed, new smuggled parts including avionic systems and NAVAIDs were installed. The new tail section with two vertical stabilizers (V shape) was designed and installed. Several new NAVAIDS such as a new TACAN system were installed as well as the old AN/ARN-84(V) TACAN system. Two K-36LT ejection seats, similar to those installed on board the F-5B Simorghes were installed in the aircraft. A new safe UHF radio, assembled by the Iranian Electronic Industries company, was installed too. Aside from these new features, no changes was performed to the aircraft's systems.

After a 12-month delay, the aircraft was prepared for the ground tests at the IAMI facility, Shahin-Shahr, in December 2014. After several test flights in January and February 2015, the aircraft was prepared for delivery.

Finally the aircraft was flown to Mehrabad international airport for an official unveiling ceremony on 5 February 2015. The aircraft, painted in the full Asia Minor II colour scheme and serialled 3-7182, was unveiled to the public during the ceremony at the airport on Monday 9 February 2015.

Between January and March 2009, the Owj Complex ran a series of test and training flights with the first three Saegehs from the IAMI airport at Shahinshahr. In April that year the aircraft were redeployed to TFB.2 and put into service with the 21st TFS. A few weeks later, the IRIAF deputy of operations ordered the re-establishment of the 23rd TFS as a unit equipped with the 'new' type. This squadron was reinforced with the fifth and sixth Saeghe in 2009 and 2012 respectively.

The small fleet has been operational ever since and has participated in most IRIAF annual exercises and gunnery rehersals, with one exception – the first Saeghe, serial 3-7366, was sent to the Owj facility in 2011 for the retro-conversion of its intakes and nose section to the original shape. During the course of this work, completed in August 2013, the plane received the same fins as those installed in all other aircraft.

MODIFICATION ATTEMPTS

Except for attempting to launch the domestic production of new F-5s, SSJD's distributed around various IRIAF air bases initiated a number of attempts to modify and upgrade the surviving F-5E/Fs. Eventually, the activities of eight such teams distributed across eight different bases around the country came under the control of one, centralized command structure – the Self-Sufficiency Department – with its own commander, the deputy of the self-sufficiency group (SSG).

Two of the first issues tackled by the SSG after the war with Iraq were the lack of chaff & flare dispensers and the lack of RWRs (Radar Warning Receivers) on Iranian F-5s. During the early 1990s the SSJD of TFB.4 ran Project Pishwa, during the course of which they installed AN/ALR-46 RWRs taken from F-4Es on the cannon access doors and the boat tails of two Tiger IIs (serials 3-7028 and

3-7093). Although the results were deemed acceptable, the project was cancelled and no further modifications were undertaken. The RWR on 3-7028 fell into disrepair over the course of the subsequent years, but 3-7093 was maintained in operational condition and was used several times for operational inspections of the IRIAF's early warning radar sites in the Khuzestan Province. Tragically, 3-7093 was lost while flown by Major Mahmood Alawi on 9 April 2007 – it nose-dived into the ground near the village of Golkhaneh, northwest of Andimeshk, while testing the newly installed equipment of the Dehloran radar site. The pilot was killed during an unsuccessful ejection attempt.

Parallel to activities at TFB.4, the SSJD at TFB.2 ran its own, projects, one of which resulted in the installation of AN/ALE-29 chaff & flare dispensers on the outboard underwing pylons of several F-5Es

S.110-001 (later 3-7366) was presented to Seyyed Ali Khameneiee, supreme leader of the Islamic regime, in March 2004.
(Babak Taghvaee Collection)

Both above: The main features of the second Saeghe were its vertical fin and removed wingtip missile launchers. They made a curved wingtip instead of the launcher, with the direction lights on that.
(photos by Babak Taghvaee)

This former SVAF F-5E had an interesting life. It was rebuilt at Owj and then IAMI and flew under the Azarakhsh name after which it was converted to a Saeghe at an IAMI installation. This aircraft with 3-7369 became the fourth manufactured Saeghe.
(Photo by Babak Taghvaee)

This unique photo of 3-7369's cockpit was taken by a visitor to the IRIAF's exhibition in 2012. It shows that the IAMI Company claims of the avionic upgrades and installation of MFDs and HUD of SR.II were not true. The former olive drab Azarakhsh colours are visible under its windshield and canopy. (Babak Taghvaee Collection)

Two years passed before the mechanics and engineers of Owj Complex returned the 3-7366 to its neutral and original shape. They replaced the square-shaped intakes with the original F-5E intakes and removed the metal inverted F-5B nose section of the aircraft and installed its original radome and bulkheads. This photo was taken while the aircraft was undergoing painting. (Photo by Babak Taghvaee)

During the IRIAF exercise Modafeane Harime Velayat-3, the 23rd TFS performed bombing and rocketry missions. This photo was taken as 3-7367 and 3-7370 released their Mk.82SE retarded bombs on dummy targets at the Shabestar gunnery range. (Photo by Babak Taghvaee)

This mix-formation flight of two 21st TFS F-5Fs (3-7169 and 3-7174) and three Saeghes of 23rd TFS (3-7368, 3-7369 and 3-7370) flew at the start of Iran's Military Day Parade in 2011.
(Photo by Babak Taghvaee)

within the framework of Project Zam Zam. However, immediately after the first F-5E (serial 3-7023) was equipped in this fashion, the plane was temporarily deployed to Mashhad AB, in northeastern Iran and this project was also cancelled.

One of most important and boldest attempts to modify the remaining F-5Es was launched in 1992 by the SSJDs at TFB.1, TFB.2 and TFB.3, and included the installation of a fixed in-flight refuelling probe (IFR) on two F-5s (and several MiG-29s). Although highly successful, this project was never pursued – the IFR probe of F-5F 3-7169 was subsequently removed, while the F-5E 3-7070 remained in place, but it was never used.

Finally, in 1994/1995, the main branch of the IRIAF's SSD launched its own project – aiming to improve and upgrade the AN/APQ-153 radar – Project Ofogh. The result of this work was improved detection range (with lock-ons obtained on targets at distances of 42 kilometres), which in theory would provide the F-5Es with the capability to engage targets from beyond visual range. However, because such an improvement would necessitate additional work on the fire-control system and required the acquisition of suitable missiles, both of which were not to hand, further work was suspended in 1998.

That said, the SSD did modify the abovementioned second Azarakhsh making it compatible with the Russian-made R-60MK

3-7303 was the new serial number of 3-7028, which was the first F-5E upgraded with RWR antennas within Project Pishwa. This Tiger II is inoperable but was considered one of the best F-5Es between 2004 and 2012. (Photo by Babak Taghvaee)

A close-up of the adapter for the PL-7 as installed on the F-5E 3-7140 for display at TFB.1 in 1997. This Tiger II was never wired to deploy these Chinese weapons. (Simon Watson Collection, via Tom Cooper)

The F-5E 3-7070 was the second Tiger II equipped with an IFR probe. The aircraft is still flying in this configuration, although not accepted for fleetwide service. (IRIAF's Deputy of Self-Sufficiency)

and Chinese-made PL-7 AAMs. However, related testing was not successful and these attempts were stopped too.

Following the failure of all these projects, a new commander of the SSD launched a new effort to introduce fleetwide upgrades for IRIAF's F-5s with the help of several Chinese and Russian companies, late in the 1990s. A number of Chinese and Russian experts for radars, air-to-air missiles and aeronautical engineers visited the Owj Complex in 2001, and – in cooperation with Iranian experts – put together an all-encompassing upgrade package known as Project Silk Road II, or SR.II. This project centred around a custom-tailored variant of the Chinese-made SY-80 fire-control system – which necessitated the installation of a slightly enlarged radome and the removal of the starboard (right) M39 cannon – the SR.II was to result in an aircraft equipped with PL-5C AAMs, two multifunction displays (MFDs), a combined GPS and JD-3 TACAN navigation platform with moving map indicator, new radar scope, new HUD, Type III IFF, Chinese-made 930-4 RWRs and 941-4AC chaff & flare dispensers, and other avionics.

The IRIAF offered the Azarakhsh 3-7301 for corresponding modifications and these were completed by 2002. An Iranian engineer recalled:

> Two of us were supervising Chinese radar experts. At some point in time they installed the radar, although there was no suitable radome for it, and then asked us to provide electricity for the system. We asked why, and they told us that they want to put the radar to the test – right there, in the middle of a hangar. Surprised, we told them this is not safe, especially not with six other technicians working in front of the aircraft.
>
> Eventually, the Chinese manufactured a new radome in China, made of composites, and this was delivered to Owj Complex. During inspection of it we found its quality so bad, that it was reducing the radar range by 50%. We manufactured a new radome in Iran, and this proved much better than the Chinese version.

An officer from the IRIAF intelligence department concluded:

> The seven Chinese experts – four men and three women – had lots of experience on Shenyang F-7 fighters, but none on F-5s, or other of our US-made equipment. They showed extremely curious to get access to our F-14s and especially their AIM-54A missiles. We prevented them from this, and did not even allow them to take any photos inside the Owj Complex. Later on they were re-located to TFB.4, and remained closely monitored. We did not allow them even the use of computers: they had to draw everything on the paper. Eventually, it turned out that under excuse of drafting a new flight manual and technical orders for SR.II, they were attempting to gather intelligence on existing

documentation for our F-5Es. They came to espionage on us, not to help. We ordered them to pack and they were sent back to China.

The work on upgrading the 3-7301 was completed and after successful testing the IRIAF assigned two additional F-5Es – 3-7034

Head-up display (HUD) as used for Project SR.II. This system was subsequently sent to the IAMI for reverse-engineering. (Babak Taghvaee Collection)

and 3-7083 – for similar upgrades. The work on these two aircraft was completed in 2004 and both were redelivered to the 41st TFS. After solving some problem with unsuitable chaff & flare cartridges, the IRIAF deputy of operations began exercising pressure on the SSD to accept the SR.II for fleetwide application. Although the deputy of logistics and support entered negotiations with the Chinese company CATIC for an upgrade of 40 F-5Es to SR.II standard, a number of IRIAF pilots and engineers began expressing their dissatisfaction with the Chinese work. After CATIC increased the price for the upgraded components, the IRIAF decided to cancel this project too.

The three modified F-5Es served with the 41st TFS for a few years longer (re-serialled as 3-7361, 3-7330 and 3-7363), but eventually had to be grounded due to maintenance difficulties, use of non-standard spares and insufficient technical documentation. Even so, all four pilots qualified on them have gained important positions within the IRIAF in recent years.

SAVING THE F-5ES

While the various SSJD teams and the industry were wasting time and resources with fruitless or partially successful projects, by 2001 the majority of the IRIAF combat aircraft and helicopters had been grounded due to a lack of spares and poor maintenance. Both of these were the result of early retirement – and in some cases the premature deaths – of many leading officers and maintenance personnel. Concluding he was unable to meet the needs of the air force for the provision of spare parts, the IRIAF deputy of logistics and support warned the government that there was an urgent need to restore the operational capability of the air force.

As described above, various companies of the DIO were in a position to provide the necessary spares. However, a lack of interest by the government and the resultant lack of funding, rampant corruption on all levels, the lack of skilled industrial managers and the know-how in handling what was meanwhile obsolete technology, made the process of opening domestic production of all necessary

3-7301 was the first manufactured F-5E under the name of Azarakhsh by Owj Complex. Modified to SR.II standard, it served with the 41st TFS for several years and is seen above the Dez Dam, accompanied by a MiG-29UB from the 22nd TFS. (Babak Taghvaee Collection)

spares practically impossible. The IRIAF made the decision to initiate yet another major effort, on its own, to obtain spares from sources directly in the USA. Incredibly, although some of this activity was stopped by US authorities – resulting in the arrest and prosecution of about a dozen US and foreign citizens – the Iranians were extremely successful.

While the full extent of this project remains secret, one detail illustrates its success. The DIO and the IRIAF acquired 23 General Electric J-85GE-13 and 60 J-85GE-21 engines between 2001 and 2011. In 2010, they almost managed to import one former IIAF/former Jordanian F-5B, which was being operated under a civilian registration in the USA. The plane in question, former 3-7007, had been sold to Jordan in 1978 and then to the USA in 1990.

In summary, this operation was successful beyond the imagination of most of its observers as well as the involved IRIAF personnel. A large number of IRIAF F-5s remain in operational service almost exclusively as a result of illegally acquired spares.

ROUTINE EXERCISES AT TFB.2

Since the mid-2000s, the revamped fleet of F-5E/Fs and Saeghes from TFB.2 primarily ran routine peacetime operations. For example, four F-5Es and two F-5Fs of the 21st TFS, and five Saeghes of the 23rd TFS participated in Exercise Zarbat-e-Zulfiqar in September 2006. Flying dozens of missions armed with dummy and live weapons, they expended hundreds of unguided rockets and dozens of Mk.82 bombs.

Between 17 and 22 October 2008, the IRIAF ran the Modafeane Harime Velayat exercise from TFB.2 as well. This saw the involvement of one F-5F and five F-5Es from the 21st TFS, three Saeghes from the 23rd TFS, four F-5Es from the 41st TFS, and about a dozen other aircraft, which also flew missions armed with dummy and live weapons against simulated targets on the Shabestar gunnery range, navigational flights and simulated interception sorties.

Between 23 and 26 June 2009, two F-5Es, two F-5Fs and three Saeghes redeployed from TFB.2 to TFB.10 at Chabahar, on the coast of the Gulf of Oman, where they ran joint exercises with six F-5Es from the 41st TFS, as well as with Phantoms and Tomcats from other units.

The IRIAF's annual gunnery competition in 2010 – Exercise Modafeane Harime Velayat-2 – saw six F-5E/Fs from TFB.2 and six from TFB.4 and their crews competing against those of units operating Su-24MKs, FT-7Ns, and F-4Es.

In September 2011 Exercise Modafeane Harime Velayat-3 was run from TFB.2. It saw the involvement of fighter bombers and interceptors from seven other bases. Eight F-5E/Fs from the 21st TFS and six from the 41st TFS flew dozens of simulated interdiction strike and SEAD missions, sometimes in cooperation with units equipped with F-4Es, FT-7N and Su-24MKs, and sometimes 'against' them.

Since 1997, improved maintenance and safety measures have prevented major accidents with F-5s at TFB.2. Although six armed Tiger IIs are held on near-permanent QRA, despite flying hundreds of operational and training sorties, not one of them has crashed or has been badly damaged in years.

However, the period of intense training activity during the second decade of the 2000s began to show negative associations too. One MiG-29, one F-4E and an F-14A were lost in three different crashes in 2012 and subsequently the high command felt forced to halve the number of sorties flown by all units.

3-7173 (c/n: Z1020) is one of five F-5Fs of the 21st TFS. Grounded for more than 12 years it was restored at TFB.2 with the help of spares clandestinely obtained from the USA in 2013. (Photo by Babak Taghvaee)

The F-5E now wearing the serial 3-7305 (earlier 3-7051) was grounded for six years because of a lack of spares. It was overhauled and returned to service in 2009. (Photo by Babak Taghvaee)

3-7174 (c/n: Z1021) is one of five F-5Fs of the 21st TFS. This aircraft was painted in Azarakhsh colours in September 2007 in order to participate in a triple formation flight with two SR.IIs in the Holy Defense Parade that year. Three SR.IIs were required for the air parade, but only two were available, but because this aircraft was painted in SR.II colours it was used as the third, fake SR.II. This photo was taken during an exercise at Tabriz in September 2011. (Photo by Babak Taghvaee)

3-7336 (c/n: U1066) participated in a gunnery competition at Vahdati AB in August 2009. (Photo by Abbasi/Kashani)

Correspondingly, no annual exercise was held, although three F-5Es from TFB.2's detachment at TFB.14 saw a temporary deployment at Birjand and participation in the exercise Modafeane Asemane Velayat-4, staged by the newly established Islamic Republic of Iran Air Defence Force (IRIADF), and another exercise staged at TFB.9. The spate of accidents – nearly all caused by human error – continued into April 2013 when TFB.4 lost one F-5F and one F-5B in two different crashes.

Presently, TFB.2 has a total of 25 F-5Es and five F-5Fs, 86 percent of which are FMC; one F-5E and one F-5F are grounded for lack of specific spares, while the rest of the fleet undergoes periodic inspections. Nearly 40 years since entering service at Tabriz AB they continue to provide a significant contribution to the air defence of Iran's northern borders.

A vital role of the 21st TFS is to provide the air defence of Iran's northeast, a task that had not been attended to since pre-revolution days. Six AIM-9J-armed aircraft provide defence in the northwest provinces. Six AIM-9J-armed F-5Es are in five- to 10-minute QRA shifts at TFB.14, while TFB.2 has two five-minute QRA F-5Es. Just one F-5E and one F-5F are not operational and await spares. Before that, TFB.2's technical team restored an F-5E serialled 3-7339 in 2011. 3-7339 has eventually been restored too. Mechanics and engineers of TFB.2 F-5 maintenance team restored the aircraft after 17,500 hours' work. The F-5E was officially redelivered to the 21st TFS on 23 February 2012.

LAST FREEDOM FIGHTERS AT VAHDATI

Located between Andimeshk and Dezful, the Vahdati AB remains responsible for the protection of the skies over southeastern Iran. Like F-5E/Fs from TFB.2, Tiger IIs from TFB.4 have participated in all major air force exercises in recent years.

Notable among these was the deployment of three F-5Fs and two F-5Es to TFB.10 for their participation in the Milade Noor-e Velayat exercise, organized between 23 and 26 June 2009. From Konarak, the Tiger IIs flew simulated long-range air strikes in cooperation with Su-24MKs from TFB.7. This exercise illustrated the poor skills of the ground crews in preparing Mk.82SE bombs, most of which failed to deploy their retarding fins – an early detonation of the weapons deployed by Colonel Qader Asadi from the F-5F serial 3-7162 caused such damage that he was forced to eject. Tragically, while ejecting at a near-stall speed, Asadi collided with the canopy frame and was killed.

Another notable difference between F-5E/Fs operated by TFB.4 and those of other units was introduced during the gunnery competition held at Vahdati in August 2009, on orders from Colonel Yaghoub Naderi. Eager to improve the morale of his young pilots, Naderi ordered his ground crews to paint eagles and tigers on F-5E/Fs operated by the 41st TFS.

Following their involvement in various other exercises, TFB.4 deployed five F-5Es and one F-5F from the 41st TFS to Tabriz for participation in Modafeane Harime Velayat-3 in September 2011.

3-7330 in its Golden Crown aerobatic display team colours back in the 1970s. (Tom Cooper's Archive)

This photo is taken by the backseat pilot of 3-7174 en route to TFB.3 for participation in Modafeane Harime Valayat-2 (Defenders of Velayat-2) gunnery competitions in August 2010. Two other aircraft were 3-7337 and 3-7335 while all were carrying SUU-20 training pods under their bellies. (Babak Taghvaee Collection)

During the exercise Modafeane Harime Velayat-1 at Tabriz in October 2008 a TDU-11/B-targeting dart unit was fired from this F-5F serialled 3-7167 (c/n: Z1014) and was shot down by an R-73E missile from a MiG-29UB (3-6303) of 22nd the FS. (Photo by Abbasi/Kashani)

While four Tiger IIs were leaving for a mission at the Shabestar gunnery range on the first morning of this exercise, the F-5E serial 3-7306 suffered engine failure due to FOD damage. With engine No.1 out the pilot tried to prevent stalling, then his No. 2 engine suffered a compressor stall and there was no option but to eject. After directing his failing aircraft toward the Azerbaijan Square – the only area beyond the runway devoid of apartment housing – he ejected safely but unconscious. The plane impacted the ground without causing any civilian casualties, while the pilot recovered and was taken to a hospital.

After this the remaining crews of the 41st TFS withdrew from the exercise.

Despite much improved maintenance measures, the F-5E/Fs from TFB.4 have experienced two major accidents since. In early 2012, 3-7307 sufered the failure of its front landing gear but the pilot managed to bring it to a stop with only minor damage to the nose section. Colonel Hossein Tahan Nazif and his co-pilot, 1st Lieutenant Morteza Poor-Habib, were less lucky – on 21 April 2013, they collided with a hill near Abdanan while flying in poor visibility; both were killed.

Today, a total of 23 F-5Es and 12 F-5Fs remain on the inventories of the 41st and the 42nd TFS, and their primary and secondary roles remain similar to those during the last 40 years. Four Tiger IIs armed with AIM-9J Sidewinders are always on QRA and are regularly reinforced by two or four F-4Es armed with AIM-9Js and AIM-7E Sparrows, usually forward detached from TFB.6.

Except for operating F-5E/Fs, Vahdati is one of the major training facilities of the IRIAF. As mentioned, from 1994 to 2009, the Iranian air force operated two training units, including the 84th Training Squadron equipped with 35 PC-7s and the 85th CCTS equipped with five F-5As, seven RF-5As, six F-5Bs, and two Simourghs, in addition to a miscellany of Chinese-made F-7s and FT-7s. The training syllabus consisted of basic and advanced flight training on PC-7s before preparatory training for either US-made or Russian-made types. Depending on the results of this process the cadets continued either on F-5s and Simourghs, or F-7s. The training on Simourgh included a total of 100 hours, with heavy emphasis (up to 30 hours) on instrument flying early on, and on combat training (air-combat manoeuvring, tactics, gunnery and bombing) during the

second phase. Upon graduation, novices were posted to operational squadrons with pilots trained on F-5s flying either F-4s, F-5s or F-14s, while those trained on F-7s flying either MiG-29s or Su-24s.

When the IRIADF was established as a separate branch of the Iranian military in 2009, the IRIAF granted it two of its bases – the never-completed TFB.5 and the recently established TAB.14. Around the same time the decision was taken to relocate the 85th CCTS from TFB.8 to TFB.4, and thus the 43rd CCTS was re-established. During the course of moving from Esfahan to Vahdati, the former training asset sent its last three RF-5As to Mehrabad for restoration but two of which were later sent to IAMI for conversion to Simourgh.

Climactic conditions in the Khuzestan Province have resulted in an interesting organization of the 43rd CCTS's operation: the unit flies almost exclusively during winter and spring when the weather is more clement. On the contrary, it is minimally active during the summer and autumn months when poor visibility and high temperatures frequently hamper flying operations. Such measures, combined with emphasis on excellent maintenance and good availability of spares, have reduced the number of accidents with F-5s and Simourghs to nearly zero. In comparison, Chinese-made aircraft suffered at least one major accident a year, primarily related to significant problems caused by notorious weaknesses of various of F-7 systems.

One exception to this rule occurred on 27 April 2011; while on finals to Vahdati, Simourgh serial number 3-7013B collided with a civilian car that crossed the runway without prior clearance by ground control. The crew managed to get their aircraft airborne again but realized it was too heavily damaged for a safe landing and ejected. Both pilots recovered without injury.

3-7171 (c/n: Z1018) can be seen three days prior its crash on 21 April 2013. Its pilots, Colonel Hossein Tahan Nazif in aft seat and 1st Lieutenant Morteza Poor-Habib, were killed. (Photo by M.H.J.)

3-7160 (c/n: Z1007) during take-off for exercise Modafeane Harime Velayat-3 at TFB.2 in September 2011. (Photo by Babak Taghvaee)

3-7021 was the first aircraft of the second batch of IAMI-manufactured Simourghs. It is rarely flown and usually stored at Vahdati AB. The main difference from other Simourghs is its Russian K-36LT ejection seats. (Photo by Babak Taghvaee)

3-7306 (c/n: U1040) which was previously 3-7052 crashed during Modafeane Harime Velayat-3 in September 2011. Its pilot ejected safely but was injured. (Photo by Babak Taghvaee)

41st TFSs are walking toward their aircraft during the IRIAF's gunnery competitions in August 2009. (Photo by Babak Taghvaee)

F-5 ACCIDENTS IN THE 1990S

After almost eight years of extensive use in the war of attrition, the Tiger IIs were suffering from structural fatigue as a consequence of the high-G manoeuvres in battle. The IRIAF's deputy of operations and deputy of inspections imposed rigid safety regulations on the flight operations of the F-5E/F fleet, especially after detection of fatigue in the main longitudinal and wing spars of the F-5E/Fs. The new safety regulations forced the pilots to adopt a cautious approach during execution of air combat manoeuvres, both in training and combat, for a short period of time until the production of structural parts, including new wings, by the Owj Industries Complex came on stream. But in some cases, due to indiscipline of pilots and even technicians, some fatal accidents occurred in 1990s.

At 1215 on 29 May 1995, TFB.2 F-5F with 3-7165 serial number (c/n Z.1012), piloted by Captain Saeed Malek-Mohammadi (instructor pilot) and 1st Lieutenant Mohammad-Ali Kiani (student), crashed in an ACT (Air Combat Training) sortie. While the pilots were practising air combat manoeuvres, they performed a high-G pitch-up, from which 3-7165 did not exit. The pilots put the aircraft into a bank to the left and then the right in order to return to base but as the aircraft was uncontrollable, they decided to eject. Malek-Mohammadi in the back seat successfully baled out but Kiani's ejection seat malfunctioned; too late for him to eject manually, he was killed instantly when the aircraft stalled and impacted with ground. The reason for the accident was fatigue and fraction in actuator, pitch and SAS parts of the aircraft elevators due to the high-G manoeuvre. After the accident, a series of NDIs (non-destructive inspections) was performed by mechanics on the parts in order to prevent similar accidents in other aircraft.

Another accident happened, this time to 3-7107 in Shiraz, on 7 July 1995. The 3-7107 (c/n U.1095), piloted by 2nd Lieutenant Homayoon Rezaiee, was one of three F-5Es from the air base flying in an ACT sortie that day. According to the mission report, when the three F-5Es entered the training zone, they performed three training manoeuvres. During the third one, at 18,000 feet, Rezaiee put his aircraft behind No.1 F-5E and announced, "Fox 2". After his successful manoeuvre, he then disengaged and requested No.1 and No.2 pilots to turn right and wait for him on the join-up. He dived to increase his speed in order to catch them, but failed to come out of the dive. His aircraft impacted with the Kuhenjan Heights near the 7th TFB's Sarvestan gunnery range and he was killed immediately.

In 1996, crashes of F-5s continued with a series of accidents such as unwanted in-flight engine shutdowns or flameouts due to low-quality J-85GE-21 compressor sectors made by DBI, but only one aircraft and one pilot were lost.

On 4 October 1997, another Tabrizi Tiger II was lost and its pilot killed due to the human factor. The F-5E with 3-7055 s/n (c/n U.1043), piloted by 2nd Lieutenant Saeed Jabbarian, impacted the Orumiyeh Lake surface due to control loss as a result of a high-G manoeuvre during an ACM sortie at 1032 local time. Later the 4th TFB crash investigation team cleared human factor as the reason for the accident because the pilot was not conscious enough to perform high-G manoeuvres due to arbitrary use of Dimen Hydrinat anti-nausea pills.

Apart from human factor and structural fatigue, ground crew mistakes sometimes caused minor accidents and subsequent damages to the F-5s. For example, on 18 September 1998, the canopy of F-5E with 3-7052 s/n (c/n U.1040) was unexpectedly jettisoned by a soldier while he was playing with the canopy emergency jettison handle in a HAS at 4th TFB.

A second canopy jettison accident happened on 21 April 1998, but this time in flight and due to pilot error, near Mashhad. The F-5E in question with 3-7132 s/n (c/n U.1120) was a 2nd TFB F-5Es

Inattention by personnel cleaning the taxiways, runways and aprons of the four F-5 operator bases of the IRIAF caused a series of FODs to the F-5s as well. In 1998 alone, 477, 384, 245 and 32 engine technical failures happened to F-5s of 4th TFB, 8th TFB, 14th TFB and 2nd TFB respectively.

Accidental canopy jettison accidents continued through 1999 when another curious soldier jettisoned a canopy of an F-5B of the 85th CCTS serialled 3-7009 while attempting to open it in a HAS on 11 September.

And finally, on 21 October, 2000, the last accident of this kind happened to F-5F with 3-7180 s/n (c/n Z.1027) when mechanics at 4th TFB jettisoned its canopy during its engine run-up after an engine change. The aircraft fuselage was damaged in three locations and subsequently caused the withdrawal of the aircraft from service, to be used for part reclamation purposes.

The IRIAF's deputy of operations managed to reduce the F-5 fleet accident rate by cutting their flights. But lack of spare parts was another factor behind this and caused a 25% decline in F-5 flights.

Lack of operable J-85GE-13 and J-85GE-21 engines brought half of the fleet to NORS status in 2002. Most of the engines, which had been sent for overhaul and HSI (Hot Section Inspection), were being returned in unacceptable condition due to low-quality maintenance. According to the USAF AFM 31-1 Maintenance Management Order, the operational rate of the IRIAF's F-5 fleet should have been 60% FMC, 10% PMC, 24% NORM and 6% NORS, but in 2001, only 52% of the F-5s were OR while 40% of the fleet were NORS, and the remaining 8% NORM. But this situation improved strongly between 2001 and 2011, and almost two-thirds of the NORS F-5s were brought back to the flight line with spare parts procured via the IAIO (Iranian Aircraft Industries Organization).

TABLE 1

Type	Serial Number	Previous Serial Number	Construction Number	Fate	Note
F-5E	3-7323	3-7023	U.1011	OR	Detachment at TFB-14
F-5E	3-7324	3-7029	U.1015	OR	
F-5E	3-7325	3-7027	U.1017	OR	
F-5E	3-7326	3-7035*	U.1023	OR	
F-5E	3-7327	3-7053	U.1041	OR	Detachment at TFB-14
F-5E	3-7328	3-7063	U.1051	OR	Detachment at TFB-14
F-5E	3-7329	3-7152*	U.1140*	NORS	
F-5E	3-7331	3-7069	U.1057	NORM	
F-5E	3-7332	3-7070	U.1058	NORM	Equipped with IFR Probe
F-5E	3-7333	3-7072	U.1060	OR	
F-5E	3-7334	3-7074	U.1062	OR	
F-5E	3-7335	3-7077	U.1065	OR	
F-5E	3-7336	3-7078	U.1066	OR	
F-5E	3-7337	3-7082	U.1070	OR	
F-5E	3-7338	3-7084*	U.1072*	NORS	
F-5E	3-7339	3-7085	U.1073	OR	
F-5E	3-7340	3-7090	U.1079	OR	
F-5E	3-7341	3-7096	U.1084	OR	In TFB.4 service since March 2014
F-5E	3-7342	3-7109	U.1097	OR	Detachment at TFB-14
F-5E	3-7343	3-7117*	U.1106*	NORS	
F-5E	3-7344	3-7116	U.1106	OR	Detachment at TFB-14
F-5E	3-7345	3-7132	U.1120	OR	Detachment at TFB-14
F-5F	3-7157	-	Z.1004	OR	
F-5F	3-7167	-	Z.1014	OR	
F-5F	3-7169	-	Z.1016	OR	
F-5F	3-7173	-	Z.1020	OR	Detachment at TFB-14
F-5F	3-7174	-	Z.1021	NORM	
Saeghe	3-7366	S.110-001	-	OR	
Saeghe	3-7367	S.110-002	-	OR	
Saeghe	3-7368	S.110-003	U.1048	OR	
Saeghe	3-7369	3-7364	R.1054	OR	
Saeghe	3-7370	-	-	OR	
Saeghe	3-7371	-	-	OR	
Saeghe.II	3-7182	3-7180	Z.1027	OR	

Note:

OR = Operational

NORS = Not Operational Ready for Supply

NORM = Not Operational Ready for Maintenance

★ = Educated Guess

TABLE 2

Type	Serial Number	Previous Serial Number	Construction Number	Fate	Note
F-5E	3-7301	3-7020	U.1009	OR	
F-5E	3-7302	3-7021	U.1004	OR	
F-5E	3-7303	3-7028	U.1014	NORS	Equipped with ALR-46 RWR system.
F-5E	3-7304	3-7046*	U.1034	OR	
F-5E	3-7305	3-7051	U.1039	OR	Restored by TFB.1 in 2009-2010
F-5E	3-7307	3-7057	U.1045	NORM	
F-5E	3-7308	3-7059	U.1047	OR	
F-5E	3-7309	3-7064	U.1052	OR	
F-5E	3-7310	3-7067	U.1055	OR	

SR.II	3-7361	3-7034	U.1021	NORS	Phased out
SR.II	3-7330	3-7083	U.1071	NORS	Phased out
F-5E	3-7311	3-7097	U.1085	OR	
F-5E	3-7312	3-7025*	U.1013*	NORS	
F-5E	3-7313	3-7119	U.1107	OR	
F-5E	3-7314	3-7125	U.1113	OR	
F-5E	3-7315	3-7140	U.1128	OR	
F-5E	3-7316	3-7146	U.1134	OR	
F-5E	3-7317	3-7147	U.1135	OR	
F-5E	3-7318	3-7151*	U.1139*	NORS	
F-5E	3-7319	3-7183	R.1179	OR	
F-5E	3-7320	3-7184	R.1182	OR	
F-5E	3-7321	3-7185*	R.1183*	NORS	Probably specified for project Saeghe,
F-5E	3-7322	3-7182*	R 1180*	NORS	Probably specified for project Saeghe,
SR.II	3-7363	3-7301	-	NORM	
F-5F	3-7154	-	Z.1001	OR	
F-5F	3-7155	-	Z.1002	OR	
F-5F	3-7159	-	Z.1006	OR	
F-5F	3-7160	-	Z.1007	OR	
F-5F	3-7164	-	Z.1011	OR	
F-5F	3-7166	-	Z.1013	OR	
F-5F	3-7170	-	Z.1017	OR	
F-5F	3-7172	-	Z.1019	OR	
F-5F	3-7180	-	Z.1027	NORS	
F-5F	3-7181	-	Z.1028	OR	
F-5A	2-7250	-	Unknown	NORM	
F-5A	2-7252	-	Unknown	NORM	
F-5A	2-7254	-	N.6402	NORM	
F-5A	2-7255	-	N.6531*	NORM	
F-5A	2-7256	-	Unknown	NORM	
F-5A	2-7257	-	Unknown	NORM	
F-5B	3-7002	Unknown	N.8031*	NORM	
F-5B	3-7003	Unknown	N.8041*	NORM	
F-5B	3-7006	3-474*	N.8046*	NORM	
F-5B	3-7009	Unknown	N.8075*	NORS	
F-5B	3-7011B	Unknown	Unknown	OR	
F-5B	3-7012B	Unknown	Unknown	OR	
Simourgh	3-7015	2-7208	RF.1008	OR	
Simourgh	3-7016	Unknown	Unknown	OR	
Simourgh	3-7017	Unknown	Unknown	NORS	
Simourgh	3-7018	Unknown	Unknown	NORM	
Simourgh	3-7019	2-7205	RF.1005	OR	
Simourgh	3-7020	Unknown	Unknown	OR	Equipped with K-36LT ejection seats.
Simourgh	3-7021	Unknown	Unknown	OR	Equipped with K-36LT ejection seats.
Simourgh	3-7022	Unknown	Unknown	NORS	Equipped with K-36LT ejection seats.
Simourgh	3-7023	Unknown	Unknown	OR	Equipped with K-36LT ejection seats.
Simourgh	3-7024	Unknown	Unknown	NORM	Equipped with K-36LT ejection seats.
Simourgh	3-7025	Unknown	Unknown	OR	Equipped with K-36LT ejection seats.

Note:

OR = Operational

NORS = Not Operational Ready for Supply

NORM = Not Operational Ready for Maintenance

* = Educated Guess

Bibliography

Babak Taghvaee, History of IRIAF's Air Bases (IRIAF Strategic Research and Studies Office)

Brig Gen. Ali-Reza Namaki-Iraqi, Col. Qasem Agfshar, Col. Mohammad Nowroozi, Col. Mohammad-Reza Arevan, Staff Sergeant Valiollah Monadi, Staff Sergeant Shahpoor Yaghoubi, Staff Sergeant Mohammad-Sadegh Badi'ee & Staff Sergeant Alireza Eshghi-Fakour, *In the Sky of Babylon: History of the Iran-Iraq War in the Air* (IRIAF Strategic Research and Studies Office, 2005)

Brig Gen. Seyyed Reza Pardis, *Dar Ghorbat Jangidim* (War Cognizance Committee of Martyr Lt. Gen. Ali Sayyad Shirazi, 2008)

Brig. Gen. Behnam Gowhar, *Theology of War: History of Iran-Iraq War in the Air* (IRIAF Strategic Research and Studies Office, October 2006)

Brig. Gen. Masoud Bakhtiari, *Beit-ol-Moghadas Offensive* (War Cognizance Committee of Martyr Lt Gen Ali Sayyad Shirazi, 2004)

Calendar of IRIAF, *Eight Years' War*, Nos. 1–8 (IRIAF Strategic Research and Studies Office, 2009)

Col. Morteza Tolouiee, 50 Years of IIAF history (IIAF HQ, 1976)

Col. Samad-Ali Balazadeh, *The Sky Was Mine* (Soureh Mehr, 2011)

Committee on Foreign Relations, US Military Sales to Iran: Staff Report to the Subcommittee on Foreign Assistance of the Committee on Foreign Relations, US Senate (US Government Printing Office, Washington, 1976)

Declassified Documents of Iranian National Archive

Declassified Documents of Iranian National Library

Declassified Documents of Iranian Parliament of Islamic Council

Declassified Documents of IRIAF's Deputy of Operations

Declassified Documents of IRIAF's Deputy of Safety Inspections

Declassified Documents of the Iranian Army's Political Conscience Organization Historical Archive and Records Centre

Deputy of IRIAF's Political Conscience Audiovisual Archive

Dr. Ahmad Mehrniya, *Air Raid Against al-Wallid* (Soureh Mehr, 2010)

Joint Chiefs of Staff, Special Historical Study, Joint Chiefs of Staff and the Development of US Policy Towards Iran, 1946–1978 (Historical Division of the Iranian Joint Chiefs of Staff, March 1981)

Staff Col. Mojtaba Jafari, *Atlas of Unforgettable Battles: Ground Forces Operations in Eight Years of Holy Defence, September 1980–August 1988* (Holy Defence Historical Research Centre of Iranian Army, 2009)

Telegrams between US Department of State and Iranian Ministry of Foreign Affairs, US National Archive

TFB.2 History at the War (IRIAF Deputy of Human Resources, 2002)

TFB.4 History at the War (IRIAF Deputy of Human Resources, 2002)

TFB.6 History at the War (IRIAF Deputy of Human Resources, 2002)

TFB.7 History at the War (IRIAF Deputy of Human Resources, 2002)

www.iiaf.net/ Maj. Farhad Nassirkhani

About the author

Babak Taghvaee is an Iranian journalist, photojournalist, historian and defence analyst, with a deep passion for aviation. He co-authored his first book, *The Modern Iranian Air Force*, which was published by Harpia Publishing in 2010. Since 2007, he has written over 70 articles on Iranian, Russian and Ukrainian military aviation. In January 2011, he convinced the IRIAF authorities to restore eleven abandoned aircraft from the defunct Ghale Morghi air force museum by transporting them to Dowshan-Tappeh airfield. Later that year he was invited to become a volunteer researcher and historian for the air force, and was one of two supervisors on the historical research project, 'Project Identity of the Air Force' in the IRIAF's Strategic Research & Studies Office before becoming an adviser to the Iranian Aircraft Industries Organization on their aircraft upgrade project. However, the following year he was arrested because of his exposé of the high level of corruption in the Iranian aircraft industry. After several months in solitary confinement, he was charged with being a threat to national security and was tried in the Islamic Revolution Court but managed to flee the country in August 2013 after being released on bail. This book is a product of the Iranian Ministry of Information historical records that he managed to hide during the period of his arrest.